Praise for NLP Solutions

"This book is a model for all future books about NLP at work (and if you know about modelling, this is the finest compliment that could be made). It opens up the often unconscious and always complex world of 'how' by showing how to build relationships, how to establish rapport, how to sell, how to coach, how to lead – and, above all, how to make a difference and how to learn as you do so. Read it, do it, be it."

Peter Honey, business psychologist and author of Learning Styles

"I believed my preferred style of learning was experiential, until I read this book. It is written in simple terms, full of real examples, and it avoids jargon in a way that makes it a joy to read. I really hope that my comments encourage you to buy this book because there is no doubt that having read it you will develop your ability to deal with, and create, positive change, not only in your business but also holistically in your life."

Brian Chernett, Executive Chairman, The Academy for Chief Executives

"Sue Knight hits the target once again. Finally we have a book focused on modelling – the key part of NLP, and not always the most obvious – for the informed leader and manager. It's crammed with great examples from actual organisations, and places NLP in context alongside MBTI, TQM and other existing ideas. The book deserves a place in any forward-thinking manager's schedule."

Mark McKergow, Mark McKergow Associates

NLP SOLUTIONS

The new business agenda of the '90s focuses on working with change and developing people's potential and performance. The *People Skills for Professionals* series brings this leading theme to life with a range of practical human resource guides for anyone who wants to get the best from their people in the world of the learning organization.

Other Titles in the Series

NLP SOLUTIONS

How to model
what works in business
to make it work for you

Sue Knight

NICHOLAS BREALEY
PUBLISHING
LONDON

To James and Alex with my love, Mum

First published by
Nicholas Brealey Publishing Limited in 1999

36 John Street
London
WC1N 2AT, UK
Tel: +44 (0)171 430 0224
Fax: +44 (0)171 404 8311

1163 E. Ogden Avenue, Suite 705-229
Naperville
IL 60563-8535, USA
Tel: (888) BREALEY
Fax: (630) 428 3442

http://www.nbrealey-books.com

Illustrations by Sue Knight

ISBN 1-85788-227-X

Library of Congress Cataloging-in-Publication Data
Knight, Sue.
    NLP Solutions : how to model what works in business to make it
work for you / Sue Knight.
        p.   m. — (People skills for professionals)
    Sequel to: NLP at work.
    Includes bibliographical references (p.).
    ISBN 1-85788-227-X
    1. Neurolinguistic programming. 2. Employees—Training of.
3. Organizational learning. 4. Organizational effectiveness.
I. Title. II. Series.
HF5549.5.T7K617   1999
658.3'124—dc21   98-51519
                                                                                                CIP

British Library Cataloguing in Publication Data
A catalogue record for this book is available from the British Library.

Printed in Finland by Werner Söderström Oy.

Contents

Foreword
by Robert Dilts

NLP *Solutions* is well written, jargon free, and pragmatic – always a winning combination. I highly recommend it.

One of the prevailing trends in the application of NLP (especially those in the area of business) has been to make NLP 'transparent' – just as a computer user should be able to use an application without needing to know or learn the computer language with which the program was coded. Certainly, most people are more interested (and appropriately so) in buying 'solutions' than they are in buying NLP. There is a delicate balance, however, between making NLP 'transparent', and deleting references to NLP altogether.

The flip side of this, of course, are those who are so 'gung ho' about NLP that they become more interested in 'spreading the word' on NLP than they are in helping to achieve practical results for their clients.

NLP *Solutions* is an example of the perfect balance between these two poles. As the title suggests, the book is about how to apply NLP to reach effective solutions in our lives. It illustrates the application of a number of powerful NLP models and methods with easy to follow, everyday cases and experiences. The result is a book about NLP, but in which the NLP is seen clearly as the means to an end, rather than the end in itself.

Perhaps most importantly, Sue emphasizes the true core of NLP – modeling. Modeling relates to the generative rather than remedial application of NLP. Remedial applications are those primarily directed toward problem solving (like pulling weeds from a garden). Generative applications are like planting seeds. They involve taking something that is working and making more of it. NLP *Solutions* is about taking what is already working in your life and making more of it through NLP. The emphasis is less on NLP techniques than it is on expanding your own capabilities; and when you expand your own capabilities, it touches every aspect of your life.

Preface

SINCE I wrote NLP *at Work*, the use of neuro-linguistic
programming has mushroomed in the business world. The
ambitions that I had when I originally set out to introduce the
concept to managers have been fully achieved. My outcomes
now are more specifically to influence the quality of leadership
in the world today and in so doing to support business leaders
who want to make the world a place that we are proud to leave
to our children and all future generations.

I have used NLP in many situations, many companies, many
countries. For this book I have chosen some of those situations
as examples of what is possible with NLP. And I have chosen
situations that especially emphasize what NLP is really all about
– the process of modeling, which is the heart of this book.

Part 1 first explains the process of modeling, and then revisits
NLP in a business context, covering some areas that were
included in NLP *at Work* as well as some new ones. It is a
measure of my interest in NLP that even for those topics that I
have revisited, I believe I have done so with new eyes, fresh
ears and some previously untapped emotions. Some of those
emotions I have sought; some came as a result of unwished for
and sad occasions, namely the death of one of my oldest friends

and colleagues Mike Woolfe, who was in my thoughts often as I wrote.

Part 2 gives case studies of companies in which NLP has been applied in specific situations, including:

- Managing relationships
- Creating learning cultures
- Team excellence
- Personal selling skills
- Exceptional tutoring
- High-performance one-to-one coaching
- Telemarketing and customer contact through call centers
- Training
- Leadership

There are many more applications I could have included and I hope you will see that NLP is not context specific, for example. There will be ideas that you will get from reading the section on leadership that are equally applicable to managing your personal development. The joy of NLP for me is that it is generic. It applies to each of us personally, at home, at work and in life.

I hope that reading these case studies will prompt you to send me some of your own and I hope that in using the examples and ideas I have included in these pages you will make discoveries for yourself. And if you do, then the intention behind NLP will be in the process of being realized.

To send your discoveries to me you can email me on **sue@sueknight.co.uk**. I look forward to hearing from you. You can find out more about what I and my team do on our web page – **www.sueknight.co.uk** – which has updates on some of the latest applications.

I have enjoyed the learning that I have gained in the process of writing this book. I hope that you do the same in reading it.

ACKNOWLEDGMENTS

Since writing a book of my own I have been fascinated with seeing to whom other authors attribute their success, and I have thought more about this since beginning this book. Who really has supported me in a way that has made a difference – who is the difference that made the difference?

Without a doubt it is my husband Spencer. When we have been in France where I do a lot of my writing, he has cooked for me and kept the stove stocked with logs so I was nourished and warm. When I used to run business writing courses years ago, one of the pieces of advice I gave to my delegates then was to write with someone specific in mind, even if they were writing for a group of people. I wrote this book with Spence in mind and that has always been an encouragement and an inspiration. He has read everything that I have written many times! And he has done so with patience, understanding and with the much-needed critical eye.

And who else? I consider myself very fortunate to have a publisher such as Nicholas Brealey. From what I know of other publishers his is a unique style. He has acted for me as a developmental editor, which has meant that he has challenged me to think, think and think again and then to write, write and write again. I would not have done this had it not been for him and the result would have been infinitely inferior. When I pass through airport lounges on my travels around the world, the books to which I am drawn are invariably his and I am flattered to be in the company of so many leading-edge thinkers and writers. Nicholas Brealey is for me a model of excellence and I am always curious to understand his strategies for knowing what is a good book and what is not.

And Gene Early, who without doubt has been a source of inspiration for me in my thinking about NLP. He has supported me in discovering my own style and has given me the ability to model for myself. It is possible to 'do' NLP in the head but not the heart. For me Gene Early epitomizes the heart of NLP in every sense of the word that I can imagine.

And last but most definitely not least, my Mum, who somehow bestowed on me the determination to do things in my own way and to keep going until I succeed – 'You'll always fall on your feet, Susan!' And I have. They are qualities that have stood me in very good stead throughout my life and are I believe crucial to the process of writing, so Mum, I thank you from the bottom of my heart.

Sue Knight
March 1999

Part One

The Modeling Process

NLP in Business *1*

When one has sought long for the clue to a secret of nature, and is rewarded by grasping some part of the answer, it comes as a blinding flash of revelation … This conviction is of something revealed, and not something imagined.

Lawrence Bragg, *Science and the Adventure of Living*, 1950

NEURO-LINGUISTIC programming (NLP) is the study of what works. It is the process of unpacking the 'how' of what we and others do, either to achieve the same results for ourselves or to teach them to others. As such, it is a process that leads to continuous growth and learning.

'So what?' a delegate on one of my training programs once asked. Well, if we understand the conscious and unconscious structure of how we do what we do, then we have choices. The choice to refine what we do, the choice to stop what we do or the choice to do differently.

The awareness of how we do what we do is the key to self-management and influence. For example, if you understand how it is that you build lasting relationships with some of your clients but not all, then you have the choice to extend what works to all situations, people and

NLP is the study of what works for you and for others

We are what we think

contexts. Similarly, if you understand how you get stressed in some circumstances but not in all, then you have the opportunity to make some new choices – you could go for all-out stress or no stress! We are what we think, and by managing what we think we take responsibility for our lives and can live in a way that enables us to realize our true potential.

We live in an increasingly unstable world and we cannot control the things around us that may knock us off course on our journey to our goals. However, what we can do is to manage the way we react to these varying circumstances. Likewise, we may not be able to control the nature of the people who are drawn to us, but we can manage the way we respond to them. We cannot control fluctuations in the economy, but we can manage the sense we make of them and our frame of mind as we do this. Our skill and our ability to manage ourselves in this way directly affect the extent to which we achieve our goals.

We can't control people or events, but we can manage our response to them

You may be wondering what happens if you do learn all these things about yourself. It may be that you already feel that you are not realizing the potential that you suspect you may possess. But what are you going to do about it? How will you develop any gaps you discover between the you today and the you that is lingering inside bursting to get out? It is all well and good to know why you are the way you are, but can a 'leopard' really change its 'spots'? The answer is it can if it wants to – and NLP is the means of learning and making just this sort of change. It is a way of learning new choices that will change both the way you behave and the influence you have on the world at large.

THE HISTORY OF MY INVOLVEMENT WITH NLP

I first heard of NLP when I attended a creative writing course in 1987. I did not know at the time I made the booking that the concepts and techniques taught on this course had been developed as a result of modeling a creative and eloquent writer. However, I sensed something different in the style of delivery of the course and on more detailed exploration I discovered that NLP was the background process. It had been used to 'model' the way the writer thought and wrote. I was also impressed by the style of the presenter, Roy Johnson (who was, I later discovered, an NLP consultant). The short after-hours introduction we got to NLP as a result of our questioning was enough for me to decide to enroll on a one-year course.

At this time the only school offering NLP courses in London was the UK Training Centre (UKTC; now no longer operating) founded by Eileen Seymour Watkins. Within a few hours of the start of the course, I became aware that I was one of the few delegates who was not some kind of counselor or therapist; in fact, I think there was only one other person in this group of 50 from the world of business.

This was to prove a significant advantage in the later development of my work, although at the time I was not sure how I intended to use NLP either in my business or in my life. I had thought it might be something that I could package and market in the UK, but it didn't take me long to discover that NLP was a much, much bigger topic than I had realized, with many more implications for me than I could ever have anticipated. Not only was I impressed by the content of what I learned, but I was stunned by the elegance and skill of the tutors on the program. These included Gene Early, David Gordon, Robert Dilts, Barbara Witney and Graham Dawes.

NLP is a much, much bigger topic than it first appears

Although the emphasis was on therapy, the underlying theme was change and personal development and the applications for the business world became clearer to me as the course progressed. However, rather than offering NLP as a package at that time, I used it to develop my own style of presentation and training. I also used the sessions on the course to resolve some of the conflicts in my own life. The result was that I found my work becoming easier and energizing. I was already running my own business and I discovered that rather than ploughing my late-night energy into written preparation, I could draw much more

*Personal growth equates to
business growth*

inspiration from the delegates on my courses and the people with whom I came into daily contact. My whole approach to business changed. As I grew my business grew and I took on associates and an administrative team. I discovered that personal growth equates to business growth.

THE BUSINESS CASE

I completed another year of training with UKTC before deciding to give myself time to reflect on further possibilities. I had found that my NLP training had transformed my own and my colleagues' approach to work. Clients wanted to know how we could achieve great results in relatively short periods of time and with seemingly little effort. It was at this point (in 1991) that I decided to pioneer the use of NLP in the business world and launch our range of public business courses.

Concepts of personal development and the learning organization have become keys to high business performance – millions of people invest in Stephen Covey's programs of principle-centered leadership, for example. Nevertheless, many training and development programs still leave delegates with the question: 'How do I make this work?' As I have already stated, NLP provides answers to exactly this question. It doesn't delve into the whys and the whats, questions already amply addressed by a myriad of other programs; NLP concentrates on the 'how'. In this way it dovetails with so much that is already on the market: Peter Senge's work on learning organizations, Myers-Briggs psychometric testing, Belbin teamwork, the leadership development programs of Hersey and Blanchard and much, much more.

Major companies such as BMW, PPP Healthcare, British Telecom, ICL, PricewaterhouseCoopers, and most of the major building societies and banks, as well as the big names in the travel business, are using NLP as the basis for their business and staff development. A leading bank in Denmark, Spar Nord, is doing the same. My company has clients in the manufacturing business and the fuel industry as well as in smaller entrepreneurial companies which are using the thinking to help them accelerate their growth and build on their already established solid foundation. In addition, HRD specialists, trainers and consultants recognize that NLP offers a way of thinking and working that keeps them at the leading edge of people development. The case studies in Part 2 of this book are examples of how NLP has been successfully used in everyday business situations.

I use NLP as the basis for my work because it is more effective than any other approach I have used. In fact, if ever there is a complaint about NLP it is not that it doesn't make a difference but rather that it *does*. One of my clients commented: 'Could you slow down the process, Sue – we hadn't expected to achieve results quite as quickly as this!'

NLP works

We look for ways of continually improving the speed and the effectiveness of what we do. For instance, on a recent IT seminar the presenter pointed out the value of being able to navigate your way around a keyboard using the keys rather than a mouse. With the keys you can save seconds on each command you make, which for the most frequently used commands can mean a saving of something in the order of half an hour a week. This adds to up to a couple of hours a month. Who would not benefit from having an extra two or more hours a month available to them? This is a simple example, but this is the scale of things that make a difference to our overall performance. Take another example: if your choice of words in a sales situation makes the difference between getting the business and not getting the business, when your product and that of the alternative supplier are indistinguishable, then the results are even more obvious.

The applications of NLP and its discoveries are manifold, but examples of what has been discovered include:

NLP DISCOVERIES

● From people, teams and organizations who consistently achieve the results that they really want – the ability to set goals that are compelling and that have a momentum of their own.

- From people who are skilled in building relationships – an approach that enables people to feel comfortable in our presence, so creating a climate of influence.

- From those who are able to resolve conflict either within themselves or for others – the ability to reconcile different and seemingly opposing points of view to find a solution that integrates both in an innovative and empowering way.

- From visionary leaders – a style of communication that is so compelling and motivating using language that is so enriched that it inspires others to be a part of that vision.

SPECIFIC SKILLS

These are just the tip of the iceberg. There are more specific skills, such as:

- The ability to choose an emotional state and hold that state for as long as you need it. These states might include concentration, confidence, enthusiasm, motivation, influence or learning.

- The ability to think creatively and to engender a culture of creativity in the organizations in which you live and work.

- The ability to speak using words and behaviors which your listeners can both relate to and understand.

- The ability to make decisions with commitment.

- The ability to listen with your whole body in a way that allows you to hear both what is and what is not being said.

For me the joy of NLP is its generative qualities. It is a dynamic learning process. The discoveries are the results of the process; they are not the process itself. If anyone has told you that the processes of building rapport, the distinctions in eye movement, the language patterns or the techniques for achieving goals are NLP, then you have been misled. They are not. They are merely the byproducts of the process. The fruit is not the tree. It should also be remembered that NLP is not a cure-all in itself, although what you do with it might be.

SOME NLP SUCCESS STORIES

- BMW wanted to reproduce the talent of its top salespeople. These were people who were able to achieve their targets consistently in sections of the market that the company now wanted to attract. Using NLP, they identified what really worked in the sales approach of these top performers and, having identified the 'difference that makes the difference', taught this way of selling to the rest of the salesforce. The salesforce achieved all the sales targets that they set themselves for the coming year.

- A team of telemarketing salespeople in Save & Prosper modeled what they were doing currently and how they got the results they did. With this awareness, they gave themselves new choices. The short-term result was that the percentage of cold calls that were turned into conversations increased by 40 percent, while the subsequent conversion of calls into sales rose by 30 percent.

- A manufacturing business analyzed those people who were most successful in the fulfillment of their roles in the business. They were able to identify a better fit between existing members of staff and the roles required in the business, with the result that the people in those roles have achieved all their targets and staff turnover has dropped by 5 percent.

- A leading consultant developed awareness of the words they used and the effect of those words when talking about the achievement of their goals. They identified how they blocked themselves from the success they claimed they wanted. To solve this problem, they introduced new choices to their thinking and their language and they have accelerated their progress towards their personal and business vision.

- PricewaterhouseCoopers wanted to know how their top project consultants achieved their consistent levels of success. They commissioned an NLP modeling project to find the answer and they incorporated the presentation of the results in one of their international conferences.

- Some of the most experienced salespeople in ICL wanted to develop their ability to build long-term relationships. They learned how to recognize the behavioral clues that indicated preferences in styles of thinking and communicating. The result was that they enhanced their sensitivity and responsiveness to their customers, even those they had already known for many years.

- An independent presenter wanted to earn a living on the speaker circuit, which involved talking to groups of 200 people and more. She modeled some of the most financially successful people who were presenting in similar subject areas to her own. Within two years she was making a living in exactly this way.

THE HISTORY OF NLP'S DEVELOPMENT

The process now called NLP began in 1972 with two Californians, John Grinder and Richard Bandler. They were curious to know how it was that some people excelled at what they did whereas others merely 'got by' or at best achieved inconsistently good results. They were both interested in therapy and hypnosis and among the successful people they admired in these fields were Fritz Perls, a Gestalt therapist, Virginia Satir, a family therapist, Milton Erikson, a hypnotherapist, and Frank Farrelly, known for his unusual yet powerful approach called provocative therapy. Grinder and Bandler's interest lay in unpacking (modeling) the approaches used by these people and others whom they admired so that they could reproduce the same consistently high levels of success for themselves.

Despite being masters of change, the people that Grinder and Bandler studied could not explain exactly how they achieved their success. This is often the way. How often have you asked someone else 'How did you do that?', only to be met with a shrug or a vague explanation that bore very little resemblance to what actually happened? And even on the occasions when you did get an explanation, this proved to be less than useful when you sought to put the advice into practice for yourself.

How did you do that?

Grinder and Bandler realized that they could not rely on the people they modeled for the answers. They decided to watch what these people did and to study their movements in detail. John Grinder was a linguist by training and brought his understanding of language patterns to the partnership. This gave them a means of listening to the nuances and patterns in their subjects' language. Richard Bandler was a programmer and a mathematician and this training in structure and sequence provided a means of coding what they studied. Between them they rehearsed what they had learned and gave feedback to each other. They found that they were able to elicit both the conscious and the unconscious processes used by their subjects and to adopt them so that they could reproduce the same results with consistency.

As they developed this approach to modeling they discovered processes that refined their methods of study. For example, they discovered that their subjects had subtle, sometimes almost imperceptible means of building rapport, both in the way that they used language and the way that they matched the behavior of their clients. Bandler and Grinder were able to use these techniques to strengthen their rapport with future models of excellence and so accelerate the process.

NLP is the study of best practice

We now have some 20 years' worth of the results of modeling available to us. Although their initial results were from the world of therapy, as interest in NLP spread to other areas we have discoveries from the fields of communication, learning and influence. And as the research extended into some of the 'harder' business areas, we have discoveries from the areas of sales, leadership and teamwork. There are of course many more discoveries and applications yet to be made. Even as I write there will be new applications of modeling that are only just being discovered. The result is that we have at our disposal numerous insights into what really works in all of these areas. We also have the means to adapt this best practice to suit our own unique circumstances.

WHAT ABOUT THE NAME?

The various components of NLP – neuro, linguistic and programming – can be summarized as follows:

Neuro

- **Neuro** refers to the neurological system, the way we use our senses of sight, hearing, touch, taste and smell to translate our experience into thought processes, both conscious and unconscious. It relates to our physiology as well as our mind and the way in which our mind and body function as one system. Much of NLP is about increasing our awareness of our neurological system and learning to manage the choices we have available to us.

Linguistic

- **Linguistic** refers to the way we use language to make sense of our experience and how we communicate that experience to others and ourselves. The study of our linguistic patterns enables us to explore how we influence ourselves and others. Our language patterns are rich in clues to how we structure our internal world.

- **Programming** is the way we code our experience. Our programs are a combination of thought patterns and behaviors influenced by our beliefs, values, sense of identity and purpose. The results we achieve and the effects we create in ourselves and others are the consequence of our personal programs. By increasing our awareness of what programs we and others run, we can begin to learn how to reproduce these programs to achieve the results we want.

Programming

The topics and approaches that I learned 10 years ago when I attended my introductory NLP training are no longer a part of my curriculum. NLP is a process of discovery and as such it is about continually uncovering new ways of thinking and working. It is a process of continuous learning and growth and is key to profound personal development. It is one of the few subjects in which I have known people to invest on their own behalf when the organizations that they worked for were not ready to back them financially. In most of the cases with which I am familiar, those same people were able to demonstrate to their companies the benefits of the training by their example and subsequently win the approval and financial backing of their management.

NLP is a process of discovery

A recognized practitioner of NLP is someone who has taken their learning and applied it to make discoveries of their own. They will have novel research and will be able to demonstrate how they use NLP to learn what they need to take them to the next stage of their personal and business growth. Since writing NLP *at Work* I have evolved in the ways in which I apply NLP. I have been invited to talk about the book and it becomes increasingly challenging to present what I thought then in the context of what I do now. This gap between the two has been another of the influences behind this book, which includes examples of the kind of work in which my colleagues and I have been engaged since the publication of NLP *at Work*.

Qualifications in NLP

At the time of writing there are dozens of registered NLP training schools throughout the world. NLP *at Work* is available in Danish, Swedish, Portuguese, Spanish, Chinese, Polish and Turkish. The term NLP and the details of some of its applications appear weekly in the many trade journals for human resource and organizational development, sales, leadership and teamwork. Qualifications in NLP are appearing as part of the job specification for any role that depends on self-management, continuous improvement, and the ability to manage relationships and achieve results through influence.

So is NLP the flavor of the month? I think not, but then you might expect me to say that. One of the most significant reasons for dispelling any notion of NLP as a fad is the amazing way it complements other forms of training and development. I have trained in Transactional Analysis (TA) and run workshops in the concept for years; I still combine TA and NLP with exceptional results. I worked with Peter Honey and Alan Mumford, developers of the Learning Styles Inventory, during my time with ICL and at that time ran extensive programs based on behavior analysis for both salespeople and trainers.

Currently in The Sue Knight Partnership we run open courses that link Myers-Briggs analysis with NLP. We are often asked to design and run programs that build on the principle-centered leadership programs offered by the Stephen Covey Organization. We use NLP to provide the 'how' to the questions posed by Peter Senge's learning organization concept. We dovetail many of the traditional selling techniques with the interpersonal side of NLP. The difficulties faced as leaders try to implement some of the visionary thinking needed as part of the outcome-oriented manager approach introduced by Reddin are overcome with the sensory-based approaches used in NLP. NLP also encompasses accelerated learning and the Kaizen principles of quality and continuous improvement. In addition, methods of positive thinking are among the thousands of discoveries resulting from the modeling process.

MY BELIEFS ABOUT NLP

As the NLP schools have increased in number and the key proponents of NLP have developed their experience, it is inevitable that different styles and emphases have emerged. Richard Bandler and John Grinder have gone their separate ways and concentrate on those aspects of their work that are their own specialities. I believe that this specialization is good, as individuals have released their respective strengths and capabilities into the applications of NLP.

This growth also has its disadvantages, as new clients to the market may expect to get the same package whenever they encounter NLP. They will not. There are some distinctly different styles, underlying philosophies and values in the way the various practitioners present their wares. What you get under the banner of NLP from me or any of my colleagues will be different to what you get elsewhere. Modeling is a profound means of managing our personal development in a way that enables us to realize our potential in the present. To achieve these far-reaching results requires courage and a willingness to experience the discomfort and pain of new learning. I hope this book inspires you to extend your interest into experiencing NLP through training if you have not already done so. The words here are intended as a taste for what is possible through experience and NLP is very definitely an experiential process.

There are very different approaches to NLP

Only you can manage your learning and growth and you have a responsibility to do so. By using NLP you can give yourself more conscious choice over what you do and the way that you act. I do not subscribe to hypnosis as a technique for business; my aim is to make our clients more consciously aware of what they do unconsciously – to make

Only you can manage your learning

the unconscious conscious and not the other way round.

I also believe that the only person for whom we can assume we have permission to make changes is ourself. And while of course I recognize that we always have an influence and that the skills covered in this book are a way of increasing the ecological effects of that influence, my belief is that if you try to use these skills to manipulate others against their wishes and real needs then at some time, in some way, they will backfire.

Become more of who you truly are

I work on the principle that everything you model is already a part of yourself, even if initially you only recognize it in others. So by engaging in a process of modeling you are not changing your personality, but rather you are becoming more of who you truly are and have the potential to be.

What we give is what we get

I believe that we have a responsibility to use our talents for the good of others, but we need first to learn to accept others for who they are. There would seem to be a certain irony in that to be able to influence anyone or anything we need to learn acceptance – starting with acceptance of ourselves. By learning to manage ourselves we can be the example of what we would like to see in the world around us and this influence starts within. What we give is what we get and what we experience is a mirror to who we are. These principles underpin everything that I have chosen to include in this book.

I have spent many holidays cycling, mostly in Provence, France. If you are familiar with the area you will know that the terrain is hilly. To enjoy cycling there it is a real advantage to enjoy the tenacity and commitment that the hills demand! Having done a lot of cycling on the flat, I found the hills less than enjoyable. My build and weight are more suited to speed than to hill climbing, whereas my husband excels on the hills. So our cycling in Provence resulted in his accelerating away from me then waiting at the top of the hill while I laboriously struggled behind. I decided that for my own state of mind and enjoyment I needed to sort out my hill-climbing technique.

I began to pay a lot more attention to the way that Spence cycled uphill. I noticed that not only could he maintain his speed on the ascent, he could also accelerate, whereas I could only hope to maintain enough momentum to get to the top. I watched the way he moved, in particular the rhythm he adopted. As I paid attention to this, I also noticed that he only looked at the ground. This was in stark contrast to my style, where I constantly and longingly looked at the brow of the hill. He never did. My rhythm faltered as I struggled to maintain my speed, whereas Spence's pace and rhythm stayed the same no matter what the incline.

The next time we were on a hill I tried to adopt the same style. There was a definite improvement in my speed, but after a while my thighs ached and the pain became a distraction. Clearly, there was something I was missing.

I asked him about his strategy and, sure enough, he reinforced the importance of maintaining a constant rhythm. When I referred to the pain, he suprisingly said he felt the same, but for him the pain was an indication that he was pushing himself and developing his personal strength. So far from disliking it, he actually welcomed it. Pain for him represented an improvement in personal fitness. He also said that as he was looking down he enjoyed listening to the sound, the regular rhythm of the pedals.

This internal strategy was quite different to my own. I spent most of the time on the hills asking myself how far I had to go to get to the top and always noticing how far I still had to go, therefore getting more and more frustrated.

The next time we cycled up a hill I stepped into his way of thinking as well as his physical style of cycling. I did what he did both *as I had noticed him and as he had explained it to me. I got to the top of the hill at the same time as he did and at the same speed, having accelerated on the ascent.*

That is modeling. This is NLP.

NLP Is Modeling 2

The only work of which we are absolute masters and which we have sovereign over, the only one that we can dominate, encompass in a glance, and organize, concerns our own heart.
François Mauriac, *Cain, Where is your Brother?*, 1962

OUR life and our work are the perfect results of who we are. You may feel that your life and your work are not what you would want them to be. Alternatively, you may feel that they surpass any expectations or dreams you may have. Whatever your experience, what you have is a perfect expression of the things that you have done with excellence to get you to this very point. Maybe you have been 'excellent' in your ability to set goals and achieve them. Maybe you have been 'excellent' in your ability to procrastinate over the significant goals in your life. Maybe your 'excellence' is in your ability to build networks and longstanding relationships. Or maybe it is in your ability to create rejection and conflict with those around you. The question is not so much what you do or indeed why you have done these things, but much more importantly *how* you do it.

Just how do you achieve the results that you do? The answer to this is what modeling is all about; it is the how that gives us the awareness that enables us to repeat our successes or to introduce new choices that will enhance the results that we get, or even to change those results.

And what of the excellence that you notice in others? Concepts such as emotional intelligence are a means of recognizing the skills and qualities that really do make a difference in our successes. In everyone there is a light of excellence. Can you see it? Your skill in noticing these qualities will influence the quality of your own life. Can you recognize the excellence in the members of your family, in your work colleagues, in your boss, in your friends, in the people with whom you come into chance contact each day? I have often found the inspiration for the talk that I was about to give from a conversation with the taxi driver who delivered me to the venue. We are surrounded by a wealth of talent if we have the means to recognize and appreciate it.

In everyone there is a light of excellence

What would you think if you were to realize that all the resources you will ever need to achieve everything you want are in your life right now? My aim in writing this book is to make that realization possible. Modeling is a way of opening our eyes and ears to the riches around and within us.

THE BEST MODEL NATURALLY

Those who excel in what they do, no matter what their interest or area of work, have exquisite modeling skills to know what works and to continually refine what works. If you take the outstanding performers in any field, you will find that they instinctively detect the 'difference that makes the difference'. Those who excel at what they do have the ability to know what constitutes the difference between good and superb.

Those who excel have exquisite modeling skills

What makes something really good to eat? What is the difference between cooking something that is merely fuel and something that is a joy to devour? It is certainly not the need to make our working more complicated, neither is it an art that we must have at our fingertips. It is simply the understanding of the little things that make something especially good; the golden savoury goo that builds up under a pork chop you have left to cook slowly in its pan; the intense flavour of the bits of lamb that have caught on the bars of the grill; the gravy that you make from the sticky bits left in the pan after you have sautéed some chicken thighs. This is real cooking. The roast potato that sticks to the roasting tin; the crouton from the salad that has soaked up the mustardy dressing; the underneath of the crust of a blackberry and apple pie, rich with purple juice; these are the things that make something worth eating. And worth cooking.

Small things matter. Such as learning when to leave alone. The piece of fish, pork or lamb left to bubble in its pan without being fiddled with will form a delectably sticky, savoury crust; one that is stirred and tinkered with won't.

Nigel Slater, *Real Cooking*

Nigel Slater is among the stars of his profession and he has a style that differentiates him from other cooks and cookery writers. His innate ability to model is a key part of what has put him at the top and what I believe will keep him there.

MODELING IN PRACTICE

Modeling is the process of observing, analyzing and reproducing the structure of particular abilities, particularly excellence.

Let us take a very simple example. This is one of the first that was explained to me by Robert Dilts, a leading developer of NLP in the world today. It was this elegant case study that was instrumental in prompting me to begin to realize the power and the importance of NLP.

Modeling is the process of reproducing excellence

Ask someone who is a good speller to tell you how they do this. It is unlikely that they will know exactly what they do. Now give them a word to spell – a word with which most people would have some difficulty. 'Phenomenon' was the one that Robert gave as his example and I will never forget how to spell this as a result of what he told us. Watch the person as they spell the word – ask them if they are sure that the spelling is correct when they have done this and watch them all the time. It is most likely that if they adopt the most commonly used successful strategy for spelling then they will at some point look up, no matter how briefly. Most good spellers visualize the word; they can see it written out and all they have to do is to look up to access it. Most people when accessing what they see in their mind's eye look up, usually to their left, although there are some exceptions to this. Some may look straight ahead, defocused – another way of accessing what is stored visually in our mind. It is a very simple strategy, but one that a good speller will often take for granted and it is most unlikely, unless they have done any NLP training, that they will know what eye movements they make as they do this.

So Robert Dilts already knew this strategy when a young boy who had been categorized as learning disabled was brought to him to see if Robert could help him progress with his learning. The boy was about 11 years old and was certainly not recognized as being able to spell. Many adult good spellers will see the word that they want to spell on something like an overhead projection screen. It is unlikely that this boy had ever seen such a thing. Robert asked him what his favorite film was and he replied Star Wars. He then asked the boy which was his favorite character in the film and he said it was the Wookie. For those of you who have never seen Star Wars, the Wookie is a large bear-like creature.

Robert asked the boy if he would be willing to play a game and he agreed. He asked the boy if he could see the Wookie now and the boy looked up momentarily and said he could. Robert asked him if he could make the Wookie put his arms out horizontally by his sides (he demonstrated this) and the boy (looking up again) said yes. 'Now,' said Robert, 'I want you to hang some letters underneath the Wookie's arm – put a P, now an H and then an E underneath his arm side by side.' He paused between each one. 'Have you done that?'

The boy nodded.

'Can you make the Wookie open his mouth?'

Again the boy nodded.

'I want you to see the Wookie open his mouth and you will see some letters come out. The first letter is N. Can you do that?'

Once again a nod.

'Now see the Wookie open his mouth again and this time the letter that comes out is an O. And again and this time the letter is M and finally as the Wookie opens his mouth again an E comes out. Have you done that?'

'Yes,' said the boy, although Robert already knew the answer.

'Finally, I want you to hang some more letters under the Wookie's other arm. First an N, now an O and now an N.'

When the boy indicated that he had done all of that, Robert said to him: 'Now tell me what letters are hanging under the Wookie's right arm' (he indicated which arm he meant).

The boy said without hesitation: 'P, H, E.'

'And now the Wookie is opening his mouth and the letters are coming out again – what are they?'

'N, O, M, E,' the boy replied.

'And now tell me the letters hanging under the Wookie's left arm.'

'N, O, N,' said the boy – who had just (without hesitation) spelt PHENOMENON.

I hope that Robert gives me license for any deviations from his actual process, but the memory of his explanation was that it was elegant in the extreme. He had taken the spelling strategy that he had modeled in others and had adapted it to fit this young 'learning disabled' boy. To whom did the label 'learning disabled' really belong?

This is a simple example of how knowledge of what works can be transferred to others in ways that work for them to.

MODELING IS A PROCESS OF INNER BENCHMARKING

I have worked with some of the top sports and business coaches in the world today. Many of them are very aware of the skills that they have and what they do to bring out the best in others. Most top athletes know how their thinking affects their performance – how, for example, if they imagine themselves playing well they will enhance the likelihood that this is exactly what they will do. Similarly, they know that, if for one fleeting moment they consider how a shot or a move might go wrong, they have set themselves on course to reproduce that mistake in practice. It is inevitable that the people who coach these top performers are even more aware of those nuances of internal and external behavior and thinking patterns than their students. And yet through a process of modeling we quickly established some key patterns in the behavior of these coaches of which even they were unaware.

The coaches were very conscious of the questions they asked and the images and words they held in their thoughts. What they were unaware of was the precision with which they built rapport with other people and the speed with which they did this. We discovered that they unconsciously mirrored the subtlest movements of the people they were coaching. They unconsciously reflected back the feelings of their trainees in the words they used and in the way they mirrored their behavior. There were many other discoveries that surfaced that made the difference between an outstanding coach and a mediocre one.

NLP includes the process of inner benchmarking

The process of modeling offers the tools to elicit these subtleties in thinking and behavior. These tools are a way of carrying out this 'inner benchmarking' – unpacking our thinking strategies as well as our external behavior. We have many approaches available that enable us to conduct traditional benchmarking procedures to compare best practice in various companies, but without access to the inner thoughts and strategies we often miss the essential pieces of what really works.

We need to be able to uncover unconscious as well as conscious processes to explore strategies for excellence.

The newly appointed managing director of a UK subsidiary of a German-owned business talked of the goals that he had set himself. He wanted the subsidiary company to become the flagship for a new culture and way of working for the whole business. However, he realized that to achieve this he first of all had to learn how to influence the German owners in a way that meant they would listen to him more and more over time.

He had already identified someone in the Swiss arm of the business that had this skill. When he was in meetings with this Swiss manager he watched and listened to see how it was that he managed to have so much influence. He noticed that the Swiss manager always repeated some of the words that the German managers used in his response to their questions. He also noticed that the Swiss manager had the same clipped end to all of his sentences and that he had similar mannerisms and ways of moving to his German bosses. Whenever the management team was in any form of negotiation, the Swiss manager never responded with a disagreement – he always started with a statement of understanding and acceptance, even if he then shifted from this point further on in the conversation. And usually at some later point he seemed to have the ability to distance himself from any emotion that existed in the conversation, to take what the MD described as a 'helicopter view' of what was being discussed.

Although the MD could not yet identify the thinking behind the Swiss manager's behavior, he nevertheless had a lot of the external key pieces that contributed to this manager's influence. The MD had already embarked on a process of modeling. With more skills and techniques for observation, listening and questioning, he would be able not only to access more of the behaviors that contribute to the Swiss manager's influence, but also the internal thinking processes that this manager used.

BORN TO MODEL

We are born with all the modeling skills we will ever need. We learn to live by modeling those around us. Children learn to talk by modeling parents and equivalent figures in their formative years. We learn to behave by following the example set by the significant people in our lives. We learn to succeed or fail by hitching ourselves to others whose patterns in thinking and behavior we unconsciously follow. 'Hitch yourself to a rising star' was the advice one of my colleagues once gave me. It was the simplest (and most effective) way he knew of encouraging me to model those from whom I could learn the most.

Unfortunately, along the way some of these instinctive skills are lost or trained out of us. Recent research has

We are born with all the modeling skills we will ever need

shown that most people have lost the ability to pick up nuances of dialect when learning a foreign language after the age of 12. The ability of most schoolchildren to learn their allocated and chosen subjects has become limited once they have spent a few years in our education system. The ones who are inspired and motivated by their medium for study are the fortunate minority. Others turn their modeling to socially less desirable skills and behaviors where their natural talents are unrestricted and allowed to flourish.

So the skills we need and want already lie within us somewhere. Modeling allows us to access those skills when we want them. For example, if you want the confidence to present a new idea to someone who is renowned for being critical, then somewhere in your experience you have that confidence. You may not have applied it in the same way as you want to now, but the structure is there. If you want the motivation to act in a way that is invigorating for you and for others there will have been a time or a context in your life when you had this, no matter how long ago or how brief. We have a wealth of resources at our fingertips once we know how to access them.

There will have been times throughout today when you have needed to draw on specific resources within yourself. What matters is how successful you were in doing this. Think for a moment about what you have needed. Have there been moments when you did not manage as well as you would have liked? Conversely, there may have been situations that you handled with an excellence that you would like to be able to access more often. From my own experience I needed to stay calm when the technology I relied on did not work. I needed to know how to balance the use of my time throughout the day so as to meet my needs and those of my husband. I needed to know how to overcome the temptation to put off what I had to do in favor of distractions. And I wanted to be able to stop what I was doing from time to time and relax in a way that allowed me to savor the beauty of the surrounding countryside. And so on. Most of these moments we manage unconsciously *and* we can always improve on the way we do this by becoming more consciously aware of just *how* we do what we do.

We can become consciously aware of how we do what we do

TUNING IN TO THE DIFFERENCE

I recently watched a television program about music producer George Martin – probably most famous for the work he did with the Beatles. In the program George Martin sought to discover what made a 'good' piece of music; in particular, what made a melody and what made music memorable and popular. The program centered on his explorations with people who had written music that met these criteria. He interviewed Paul McCartney, Stevie Wonder, Billy Joel and Brian Wilson. He studied the harmonies and melodies of music by Mozart and Tchaikovsky. What was fascinating was that he was modeling what really works and even more fascinating was that the composers he spoke to felt that there were some pieces that seemed to fit a formula that even they could not explain. And there were some, Paul McCartney included, who did not want to be able to explain. The score for *Yesterday* came to him in a dream!

However, although George Martin could not pin down all of the elements that made a difference, he did find some of the factors that set some famous pieces apart from the rest. He did discover, for example, that the successful pieces had a very simple melody at their core and that this melody followed a characteristic pattern in terms of falling and rising notes. What was also consistent in the composers' explanations was that they all felt that there was something unexplained that came from the heart or the soul.

During the program the interviewees commented on what makes a good composer. One of those interviewed said that the best composers studied life; they analyzed what was happening around them every day. The best of these could condense what they discovered into a simple melody. The best in any profession, and especially those

Modeling is an attitude to life

who continue to be the best, have this skill of modeling. And it is much more than a skill – it is an attitude to life. If you want to be the best at what you do and in particular if you want to get lifelong discovery and enjoyment, then modeling is a very significant part of the answer.

THE NEED TO MODEL

Our ability to learn is related to our ability to survive

We live in a world where there is an ever-increasing rate of change. We live in an insecure and often violent environment, in which there are many unresolved conflicts. Consequently, we can no longer rely on others or our organizations to look after us – we have to be able to care for ourselves. We have to be able to manage our own development however benevolent our organizations may be. Research shows increasingly that our ability to learn is directly proportional to our ability to survive and succeed. Indeed, I believe that it is only by developing our ability to learn that we can hope to stay ahead in what we do and ultimately lead the way. I quote one of my clients:

We do not have any more hours in the day and we cannot pour any more resource into what we do. I have come to the conclusion that we need to think differently.

Courses and books are incapable of providing us with the skills that we require for every eventuality – a new need emerges every few moments. The rate of change demands that we are able to learn in every moment of the day; we need to be able to draw learning from everything we experience, good or bad. We need to learn from everything and everyone.

HOLISTIC MODELING

A holistic approach to modeling

My approach to modeling is holistic. The purpose of this kind of modeling is to integrate all the parts of ourselves so that we can be who we truly are. It is to strip away the shell, the wrapping on the present, the mask that hides our true selves from the world in order to be the successful, whole self that is within. I believe that only in this way can we be fully successful, knowing what we really want and releasing the potential that can otherwise be locked away and untapped.

Someone came up to me at the end of a talk I was giving and told me that she had modeled so much from others that she had lost the true sense of her own identity. With holistic modeling the opposite is true – you gain a greater and greater sense of self. My aim is that the more you use the principles I have explained in this book, the more aligned you become with your true self.

We differentiate by being uniquely who we are, by realizing our own distinct talent and by allowing our very individual outcomes to unfold.

We differentiate by being uniquely who we are

Our potential modeling subjects surround us. By modeling the qualities we want from others, we begin to integrate them for ourselves and in so doing we gain more conscious choices in what we do. In this way we can grow our influence, not only in the everyday situations that we face but also with ourselves. This influence enables us to grow in personal stature, in our ability to relate in loving ways to others, and in our ability to make decisions that are of genuine benefit to all the people for whom we care including ourselves.

WHAT YOU CAN ACHIEVE THROUGH MODELING

Once you have mastered these skills, there are many ways in which the results can be applied. These include:

1 To unpack what it is that 'really works'
We exist in a world where the differences between those who excel consistently and the rest are now minimal. The difference between the performances of the top athletes, the top golfers, the top cyclists and the top racing drivers can be measured in fractions of a second or in percentages of points. We have these same minimal advantages in business today. These discriminating differences are

managed by unconscious moments of thought that constitute what really works. NLP provides the means to unpack these moments as if in slow motion and reproduce them at will.

2   To transfer those abilities to others, including yourself, in an integrated, appropriate and authentic fashion

It may be that like the MD mentioned earlier, you are aware of new skills that you need and you recognize others who have those skills. The more skilled you are in your ability to unpack those skills, the more chance you have of taking them on board for yourself. You may want to literally copy the approach you admire or you may want to adapt it in a way that is more appropriate for you and your circumstances. You have that choice.

You have choice in the way you use what you learn

3   To access the talents and skills that you have within so that you can be consistent in your ability to tap into them when needed

Sometimes you have resources that you don't recognize because you may have used them in a totally different context to the one in which you want them right now. For example, supposing you want the tenacity to stick with a particularly difficult job to see it through to completion. You may at one time have been tenacious in your ability to stick with a point of view, even though it was unpopular at the time and may not even have been appropriate. Some may have called it stubbornness then – but you have in that stubbornness the structure of the tenacity you want now.

4   To coach someone to have more conscious choices in work and life

To be aware of what you do and how you do it is to have choice. So often the learning we most need lies in areas of which we are unaware. We don't know what we don't know. Have you ever seen yourself on a video camera and discovered habits that you never knew you had? And now

We don't know what we don't know

that you are aware of them, you begin to realize when you do them. This leads to choice. High-quality feedback of the sort that you can elicit when you model with skill is at the heart of non-directive coaching. Most of the one-to-one coaching sessions that I give are modeling sessions. I model what my client is doing and I feed it back to them – simple and powerful.

5 To elicit unique skills that are peculiar to your personal and work needs

There will be specific, unique skills that are peculiar to your work circumstances and to your personal style. No book or course can give you the exact form of this skill – only you can find it from within yourself and from your experience.

6 To spot talent

Interviewing techniques have tended to rely heavily on paper qualifications and more recently on psychometric testing, but these assume that the person you want applies for the job. Most people do not recognize the talent they have. Some of the outstanding performers in the world today are not people who came up through the traditional routes of education. More often than not, they are people who because of a variety of circumstances have realized that they have a talent for something quite different from their expected or traditional career path. Talent spotters in all fields (if they are good ones) are people who recognize the ingredients of success. They see a move or a word or a set of actions that they know constitutes the magic that makes the difference.

A skilled talent spotter is someone who can see beyond the obvious. Modelers are excellent talent spotters.

So modeling answers the questions that we face as we move in a world where we experience tremendous changes in the way we are expected to work. I recently heard it said that the skills of a typical office worker today would be almost entirely redundant within two years; this prediction

Modeling answers our questions

applies not only to office workers but to every one of us. We will all be redundant if we do not continually learn and evolve new ways of thinking and working. We need to be able to hitch ourselves to the rising stars that we experience in our lives in such a way we absorb their excellence into whatever we do. And we need to be able to recognize how we too can be rising stars wherever we are and whatever we are doing.

THE TRUE OUTCOME OF MODELING

CELEBRATING
EXCELLENCE

Modeling is a means of celebrating excellence. How often do you pay attention to those things that are going wrong and that cause irritation, as opposed to those things that are a source of wonder and delight? If it is possible to change your emotional state by how you direct your attention, then it is possible to change whole cultures by finding causes for celebration. I write this in the aftermath of France's winning the soccer World Cup and there is every reason to believe that this celebration will have an impact on the French economy and sense of success. The shift takes place in our heads and in our hearts before it ever takes place in our environment.

A friend of mine was made redundant. She was 45 years old at the time. She had applied for many jobs and became depressed with the lack of success she experienced in this process. By the time I saw her again she had come to believe that there were no opportunities for someone of her age. She called at my house at a time when I was meeting informally with some of my clients and we had taken a break for lunch. My friend joined us and chatted to the other people. Her general demeanor was one of depression and hopelessness. At one point in the conversation she commented: 'I have come to the conclusion that there are no jobs out there.' Unbeknown to her, one of the clients there had a vacancy for exactly the kind of work for which she was qualified. This fact emerged in a conversation we had afterwards, when my client explained the turmoil he felt knowing he had this vacancy but not being able to reconcile the downbeat attitude of my friend with the lively, outgoing style of the team in which the role was vacant. Far from there not being any jobs available 'out there', one was right in front of her and she was not in a state to know it.

This incident highlighted for me the way that our internal state influences the results we achieve and how our beliefs determine our experience. It is our state that either opens the door to opportunity or conversely keeps it locked out. I believe that the opportunities are always there. The question is whether or not we are ready to take them.

So modeling is also a way of influencing our state and consequently the opportunities that we attract to us or not as the case may be. By paying attention to the excellence that exists in all our lives, we can influence our perceptions and the effects we have on those with whom we live or with whom we come into contact on a daily basis. This is just one of the byproducts of what is on offer here – a significant benefit.

On the evening of the seventh day, when God had finished creating all manner of things, he took the Key to the World in his august hand and he determined to imbue Man with the obsession of finding it. To make the search challenging, he started looking for a very subtle hiding place.

To this end, he consulted all his counselors. One suggested that God hide it in the deepest part of the deepest ocean, while another proposed that he set it on the highest peak of the highest mountain, and yet another, that he place it on the darker side of the moon. But God was not convinced by any of these suggestions.

God reflected for a very long time and finally assembled his heavenly court, which he addressed as follows, 'Thank you for your recommendations, all of which I have found to be excellent and well conceived. I have decided, however, to put the key in a place which is both very near and very far away, where mankind will doubtless search for it the least.'

And he placed the Key right in the Heart of Man.

THOUGHT PROVOKERS

1   What talents have brought you to where you are in life?

2   What aspects of yourself have led to your not achieving some of the things you want in life? How could these aspects be redeployed so that you use them to achieve what you do want instead of what you don't?

3   Who have been your 'rising stars' in life? (Those people to whom you have hitched yourself at various points and from whom you have learned some of the skills to which you owe your current experience?)

4   To whom have you been a 'rising star'? Was this a conscious or unconscious choice on your part? And was the other person's choice to hitch themselves to you conscious or unconscious?

5   How do you currently manage your personal development? Is this an infrequent, frequent or continuous process? What would you like it to be?

6   What is the most recent significant learning for you and how did you go about that learning?

3 *How to Model*

The most important words printed on the map of human experience are terra incognita – *territory unknown.*

Daniel Boorstin

To model yourself, someone else, a team or an organization means to be able to reproduce the way your subject thinks, acts and feels. And it is the ability to do this with the same sequence and combination that gets the results you consciously want to achieve for yourself and possibly teach to others. The difficulty is that few people consciously know how they get the results they do. This is where NLP comes to the fore – it incorporates a growing kitbag of tools to help you find out.

For example, most people are not consciously aware of their thinking patterns as many of these are fleeting and taken for granted. However, their body does know. Indeed, we say in NLP training that mind and body are one. Our non-verbal behavior gives away clues as to what is happening inside our heads all of the time. Our eyes especially indicate what is going on in our thinking. A simple example is that when we create a picture in our

Mind and body are one

heads, we typically look up, often to our right. On the other hand, if we are saying something to ourselves then we often look down and to our left, if only momentarily. In the Appendix there is a summary of the most typical eye movements and what they mean; the subject was covered in more detail in NLP *at Work*. By watching someone as they relive how they achieved a result, you will see a sequence of eye movements that tell you how they are thinking. They don't tell you *what* they are thinking – this is not a way to read someone's mind – but they do tell you the structure of their thoughts.

Eye movements communicate how we are thinking

In NLP at Work I *tell the story of when I was faced with a room full of engineers who had been forced to attend a change program organized by their site managers. These 'long in the tooth' engineers were resistant to any idea of change and resistant to me even attempting to facilitate the process; or that is what I believed. I had learned much of my craft from another consultant, Charles, with whom I had worked both in my employed days with ICL and independently. He was superb in his ability to bring similar groups of engineers round to an open, responsive state. So faced with a room that was slowly filling with the last batch of delegates who had avoided all previous programs, I brought to my conscious thinking all that I had learned from Charles. And bit by bit I stepped into his shoes, as the result I wanted was one that I knew he could get.*

I wanted Charles's thinking of how he managed that moment between the engineers walking into the room and them taking their seats. I had to guess some of the thinking, but having worked with Charles for many years I felt I would not be too far from the mark if I guessed what I didn't know for sure. What I assumed based on what I had observed was as follows.

What Charles would be thinking would include:

- *We are we going to enjoy ourselves in the next few days.*
- *We are all going to learn things that will benefit us all, no matter what our goals.*
- *These guys know more than they often let on; it is they who really manage what happens on the company site.*
- *These guys have got talents that they can bring into play when*

they choose and probably these talents aren't recognized or respected by some of their line managers.

- *I can show them how to get more of what they want in a way that fits with where the company wants to go, and I can learn more about what this company needs than I can from any of the line managers.*
- *I know what is important for these guys in their world at both work, leisure and at home and I am up to date on every sporting fixture in which they are likely to have an interest.*

This thinking would probably already have taken place in Charles's mind and his attention would be on watching and listening to everything that these engineers did and said as they took their seats. What he would be looking for were the one or two leaders of the group. What Charles would have believed would have included:

- *These guys have got all the resources they need.*
- *Everything they do and say contains clues for me about what is important to them.*
- *I am the best consultant to handle these kinds of workshops as I understand where the participants are coming from.*
- *It is imperative to treat everyone with respect.*
- *I am constantly learning.*
- *Everything I do and say is purposeful and there is a best choice in every moment.*

And his behavior:

- *He would smile and greet everyone with a handshake and direct gracious words of welcome.*
- *His attention was only with the delegates and he would look and listen to every detail and every nuance in how they appeared and how they spoke.*
- *He would never put his hands in his pockets or the like and would be absolutely upright in his bearing and his posture. Everything about him would be aligned.*
- *He would use a sporting metaphor to make the learning points and the sport would be one that was current in the delegates' thinking.*

If you have read my previous description of this event in NLP at Work, you will know that when I adopted Charles's way of thinking and acting it worked. I got the result in terms of the state I wanted to be in. It didn't matter whether I was absolutely correct in what I had read into Charles's behavior. What mattered was that it worked.

WHERE DO WE GET OUR INFORMATION?

In the case of Charles, I had got the information by sitting alongside him in very similar situations on numerous occasions. I had also drawn information from what he had said to me over time and from what I deduced to be the case given the way he acted. It is likely that, given the choice of who we want to work with, we would all mostly choose people we admire. What NLP gives you is the conscious ability to elicit what these chosen exemplars do and, more specifically, how they do it.

However, you may not always be fortunate enough to be able to work with those you admire most. As a result, you may have much less time with the people you want to model. It may be that they only grant you a few hours or moments of their time. Then you need to be able to model with speed. How can you make the best use of the time?

- Decide what it is that you want to model. I heard of a teacher recently who wanted a skill very similar to the one that I wanted from Charles. This student teacher wanted to be able to enter a classroom and command the attention of the children in exactly the same way as one of the most respected and experienced teachers in the school. Decide how you will know when you have the skill you want.

What do you want to model?

- Don't waste time listening to them telling you what they do. Either ask them to do whatever it is that you want to model so that you can see them in action, or have them relive it in their thinking. You want them either actually experiencing whatever skill it is that they have and you

Have them do it or relive it

want, or you want them going through it in their thinking as if they are doing it right now. You do not want them to analyze what they are doing and how they are doing it (unless you feel they have sufficient awareness to engage in this self-modeling process); that is your job. You only have to test this out by watching someone tell you how they spell PHENOMENON and compare this with their behavior when they actually spell it. If you contrast their eye movements between the two activities you will see the difference.

Watch and listen

- Watch and listen to everything the person says and does. Watch the movements of their eyes, their mannerisms, their gestures and their posture. Listen not only to what they say but, even more significantly, to how they say it. Listen for voice tone, emphasis, pauses, volume and speed. Watch and listen for patterns, similarities and differences in what they do and what they say.

Notice the details

- Notice how they manage their environment – where they sit or stand, how they arrange their environment around them or not. Everything that they do says something about them. Modeling is about learning how to notice the details and how to make sense of them.

Get feedback

- If appropriate, try out some of what you think they do while you are with them, so that they get a chance to correct you if they think they do or think something different. You may sometimes model people remotely – they may never know that they have been the subject of your study, in which case feedback from them is not an issue.

Everything is a metaphor

- Assume that everything is a metaphor. As Tom Peters said in *Passion for Excellence*: 'Coffee stains on the flipdown tray [in an aircraft] mean they don't do their engine maintenance right.'

WE ALREADY KNOW

We already know how to model. This is how we learn to speak, to walk, to sing, to cope, to achieve what we want. Some of us do this more successfully than others. It is not unusual to find that people in positions of most influence are skilled in their ability to model. These key influencers have watched and listened to those around them throughout their lives to learn what they need to know to get what they want. This skill emerges in childhood. If you have children, you are probably very well aware of the strategies they use to get what they want. And there will be some strategies that are more successful than others.

The skills start in childhood

We model to get the basic skills we need in life. Sometimes we choose inappropriate subjects, people whose skills may not be socially, ecologically or politically acceptable in others' eyes.

Sometimes we model consciously but more often than not we do it unconsciously. A colleague of mine said that he left his previous company because he did not want to acquire the style of the managers there. He felt that if he stayed there long enough he would become like these managers whom he did not respect – so he left before there was time for this to happen. How often have you found yourself unconsciously modeling skills that you would not consciously have chosen to acquire?

For most of us there are infinite ways in which we can consciously learn to acquire the skills we want with more precision and speed. The more we manage our ability to model, the more we manage our ability to learn and to achieve the things that are important to us in life.

One of the managers charged with facilitating change in a large, bureaucratic establishment said he wanted to form a ginger group – a group that would explore what they needed to do to achieve the vision they have for the future. He explained that if they did form this group, he wanted to invite people from other organizations who had already succeeded in the areas that the organization wanted to change. 'I want to learn from people whose experience and success match our goals and our needs,' were his words.

His ability to do this would depend on his ability to model. The more skilled he and his colleagues were at modeling, the more they would elicit from their guests what really was the 'difference that made the difference'. Without this skill, it is likely that they would miss some of the key elements of what truly made this difference. With modeling skills, they would elicit elements that even the guests themselves could not quantify.

This book offers you different approaches to modeling. In reading them you may find that you develop more of your own – that is the idea, and that would be a measure of the success of what you read in these pages. I would love to know what further methods you find work for you – and maybe I will be calling you for your permission to include them in another book! If the modeling that you do is generative and creates learning, then you are on the road to continuous learning.

WHAT ARE THE ELEMENTS OF MODELING?

WHAT DO YOU WANT TO MODEL?

There are many different ways of modeling and it really does not matter which one you use as long as you achieve your goal. You need to know first of all what you want to model and why, so that you will you know when you have succeeded. You also need to know how to begin and then how to finish the process.

TOTE

You may find the model in Figure 1 useful for this, the TOTE (Test – Operate – Test – Exit).

We live our lives as a series of TOTEs. Something triggers us to do something – to want or to need to achieve a result. The sorts of triggers we experience in our everyday lives include:

- The phone rings
- We feel hungry
- A baby cries
- We are invited to do a presentation to a few hundred people
- An error message pops up on our computer screen

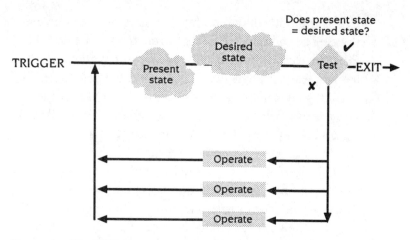

Figure 1   The TOTE (Test – Operate – Test – Exit)

- We remember we promised to do something for someone
- We make a decision to have a quiet evening at home
- We decide to write to a friend
- We hear a noise
- We set ourselves a goal for a piece of work
- A member of our family asks for some help
- We feel cold
- Our alarm rings
- We notice something unusual outside
- We become aware that one of our colleagues is upset
- A car slows in front of us

All of these are everyday examples of triggers – things that prompt a reaction. What we have to decide is what action we take. With many of these sorts of triggers, we rarely think consciously about what that action might be – we just react in a way that we have learned works. For example, when you were first learning to drive you probably had to think consciously about every move you made and every reaction you had. But after a while you learn what works; you learn what gets you the result that you want. Those conscious choices get 'wired in' so that you begin to make them unconsciously.

The pattern of learning

This is the pattern of learning. We start by not knowing what we need to know, possibly because we have not needed this particular skill before – if you have never seen a bike you will not know that you don't know how to ride one! Then something happens and we discover that we don't have the skill we want. This awareness is nevertheless a step on the learning ladder. We are conscious of doing something in a way that we don't want to.

If you have ever seen yourself on video giving a presentation and discovered that you grimace when you don't know the answer to a question, or that you say 'you know' in virtually every sentence, or that you scratch your head when you are thinking, then you will know that there is usually a time when you continue to do these things even though you don't want to. You will have become painfully aware of your incompetence in behaving in the way you want to behave. But with practice of the behavior that you do want to use, you integrate the new choice into your repertoire and it becomes an unconscious part of what you do and who you are (see the learning levels model in Figure 2).

Often what we want to model is at the level of unconscious competence, because we choose skills that others or we do automatically. It is often the automatic nature of the skill that contributes to its elegance. The aim of modeling is to elicit all elements in the sequence in which we use them that gets others or ourselves the result that we want to reproduce.

Exit points

The TOTE includes an exit point, which is when we know either consciously or unconsciously that we have achieved what we want. Of course, there may be times when we have misjudged this. Think of the salesperson who does not pick up the signals that they have sold and who keeps on selling when they should bring the conversation to a close. They have an exit point – it is just that it may not be the same as that of the customer.

Examples of exit points include:

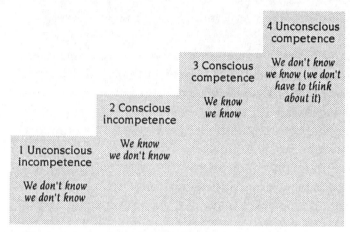

1 We don't know we don't have the skill

2 We know we don't have the skill

3 We know we have the skill and we consciously have to practise

4 We forget about the skill and use it unconsciously with ease

Figure 2   The learning levels model

- We put the phone down
- We feel satisfied with what we have eaten
- Our baby falls asleep
- We stand in front of our audience feeling confident and assured
- We are able to continue working on our computer
- We do what we promised to do
- Our customer says 'yes' with a smile on their face
- We go to bed satisfied we had the evening we wanted
- We sit back pleased with what we have written
- We identify what the noise is that we heard
- We achieve our goal
- Their problem is solved
- We feel the temperature we want to be
- We get out of bed
- We can explain what has happened
- We get an explanation that we believe
- We stay clear of the car and drive safely on

When one TOTE is complete we start another, or we may have several running simultaneously – some long-term TOTEs, which may include some of our life goals, and some short-term ones, some of which may last only a few seconds.

The operations are what we do to reach an exit. And we keep on carrying out operations until we exit. Consequently, the more choices we have in the operations we carry out, the more likelihood there is of us reaching the exit. If the operation we carry out does not get us to the exit, then we keep ourselves in a loop.

The more choices we have, the more likely we are to succeed

If we do what we always did, we get what we always got.

So if what we are doing is not working then we need to do something else – anything else will at least break the loop. Some people live their lives in loops without ever finding those new choices that will take them to their exit.

When each operation is complete we have a checkpoint – does the result that we have now match our conditions for knowing that we have what we want? If yes, we exit – we have succeeded in getting what we want or where we want to be. If no, we either go round the loop some more or we try something else – a new operation to see if that gets the match that we want. The clearer you are in knowing how you will know when you have what you want, the more able you are to reach the exit, to complete successfully.

KNOW WHAT YOU WANT TO MODEL

Precision is the key to modeling. The more precise you are in knowing what it is that you want and why, the more likely you are to get exactly what you want. And the more likely you are to know when you have achieved it.

So how do you decide what it will be? Some of the criteria that you can use to make this decision are the following:

- What personal qualities or skills do you need to accelerate your business or personal success right now?

- What obstacle (internal or external) is preventing you from achieving what you want?
- If you had it, what quality or skill would benefit you and the other key people in your life, whether at work or at home?
- What have you observed or heard or sensed in others that you wish you had for yourself?
- What is something that when you consider the possibility of having it you feel really excited or emotional, i.e. what is something to which you already feel really attached, something that is compelling in its attraction for you?

Each of the chapters that follow is an operation, a choice that you can employ to achieve what you want. And within each of the approaches to modeling there are further choices. Use whatever works for you. Initially, it is valuable to develop skills in each of the areas described, then you will have it as a later choice. The questions at the end of each chapter are designed to help you to do this. However, there is no substitute for practice and experience.

And then there was the story of the frog who lived in a dark well all his life. One day a frog from the sea paid him a visit.

'Where do you come from?' asked the frog in the well.

'From the great ocean,' he replied.

'How big is your ocean?'

'It's gigantic.'

'You mean it's about a quarter of the size of my well here?'

'Bigger.'

'Bigger, you mean half as big?'

'No, even bigger.'

'Is it ... as big as this well?'

'There's no comparison.'

'That's impossible! I've got to see this for myself.'

They set off together. When the frog from the well saw the ocean, it was such a shock that his head just exploded into pieces.

The Tibetan Book of Living and Dying

THOUGHT PROVOKERS

1. What is something that you feel you need in your life right now – a skill, a behavior, an inner strength, patience, an ability to say what you really want, a sense of purpose, motivation? Where in your own life have you had this quality? Who else do you know who has it?

2. How will you know when you have this 'something' in the way that you would really like to have it?

3. What will having this quality do for you and for the other people in your life?

4 Thinking about Thinking

What condemns us is not that thoughts enter into us but that we use them badly; indeed, through our thoughts we can be shipwrecked, and through our thoughts we can be crowned.

Desert Fathers and Mothers (anonymous sayings)

Imagine the following:

You have done what you consider to be a good six months' work. On the whole, you have achieved the targets that you set for youself and that were set for you by your immediate line manager. There were some problems along the way, but as soon as you realized this you took action and got the projects back on track. You learned from these situations so that on subsequent similar projects you raised the level of achievement and exceeded your own and others' expectations. Not only have you learned from those situations when there were some problems, but also you especially learned from those situations when you succeeded. You learned what works and what to build into your approach for the future.

Now your performance appraisal discussion with your line manager is due. You are feeling pleased with your results and looking forward to this discussion, as you would really like to move on to some more challenging projects in the coming year. You have prepared some thoughts on what you would like to cover and the time for the discussion arrives. Your manager opens the discussion with a review of your key areas of work and the targets that you were set. Rather than exploring what you have delivered, you find that he wants to analyze the one result that you didn't achieve rather than the many in which you were successful. You find this dispiriting and your energy levels drop. You move the conversation on to the areas where you have been successful, but your manager only spends a short time on these. You leave the discussion feeling demotivated and upset.

What has happened here? Unfortunately, this kind of situation can often happen in performance appraisal discussions. I have worked in many organizations where the best-designed performance management systems backfire because of the way they are applied. Several factors can come in to play, but one of the patterns that has the sort of result described above is the manager's desire to explore where the jobholder's performance has not matched expectations rather than where it has. This can stem from a belief that you need to build on problems to achieve performance improvement. But if the manager's style is to **mismatch**, then they will search for occasions when there is a difference between what was expected and what was delivered. The result of this for those people whose style it is to **match**, i.e. to look for how they did meet expectations, is demotivation and disillusionment.

Our choice can motivate or demotivate

This simple choice of inappropriate style can have serious consequences. However, having this knowledge helps us to find out what is happening and therefore to decide what new choices the manager can make to achieve a constructive result. Understanding the **filters** we use in our thinking, language and behavior enables us to model the experience and to develop our awareness.

In the situation above, mismatch was not the best choice of behavior to achieve the result, although there may be times when it is. I recently completed a teambuilding event in which the delegates told each other what they valued in the contribution that each brought to the group. One of the team members said: 'Can we now explore what I don't bring as I would find that much more interesting.' His preference was to mismatch.

WHAT ARE FILTERS?

I dedicated a chapter in NLP *at Work* to the topic of filters and that book also contains a questionnaire that can enable you to begin to understand their effect in your work and in your life. Since writing that book, I have realized the significance of these filters again and again in the situations that I face.

What sense do you make of your experience?

Pay attention to your own situation. What is true for you in your life and in your work? What state are both in? What is your experience? What are the key issues for you in life? What do you appreciate and what would you want to change? The way in which you answer these questions determines not so much what happens or what has happened to you in your experience, but what sense you make of it.

In *The Seven Habits of Highly Effective People*, Stephen Covey says that between every stimulus and every response there is a gap in which you have a choice as to what meaning you put on what has happened. The stimulus may include someone speaking to you in a way that you don't like, someone doing something that you have repeatedly asked them not to do, an unexpected event that you didn't anticipate, someone giving you praise out of the blue, a break in the clouds that lets the sunshine through on a rainy day, a loss, a windfall, a world crisis, a child's cry. It could be anything. The question is what you *do* with this event. In the moments after the event has occurred (and these may be split seconds, but then again sometimes they may be years), what goes on in your thinking? It is the meaning you put on what happens that influences your response and your reactions.

You can influence your response

Every moment of every day is a choice for you – a choice as to how you respond and consequently how you feel. These feelings will in turn influence how you act and how you influence that event and others and the people with whom you live and work.

Every moment in every day we are rippling out from ourselves emotions, expectations, beliefs, needs, values and attitudes. These ripples may be experienced as bouquets or brickbats. What you give out influences what you get back – it is your choice. Part of what determines how we receive these events are the filters that we use to make sense of what is there. Filters are what we use to decide what we pay attention to and what we don't, what we let in and what we keep out.

Every moment of every day is a choice

The manager in the case study at the start of this chapter paid attention to how the jobholder's performance did not meet (mismatched) the expectations rather than how it did (match). No matter what the intention, it is the filters we use that affect the way we behave and the results we get. **So filters are patterns in our thinking and consequently our behavior that enable us to model what is happening and how we have the experience that we have.** To get this understanding for ourselves or for others is to coach ourselves through our awareness of how we make our experience what it is.

Kevin had spent several weeks developing a project proposal for one of his key clients. He had been continually referred upwards through the organization for approval and final authorization and had successfully gained the support of everyone he had met. Throughout these preliminary stages he had built up an image of the CEO; it was a favorable one and he was looking forward to this last meeting. He knocked and entered the CEO's office and held out his hand, expecting a handshake. The CEO barely looked, kept his back partially towards Kevin and made the briefest of handshakes only when prompted for a second time. Kevin was surprised and a bit annoyed. This annoyance grew as the meeting proceeded.

He showed the CEO a PowerPoint presentation of the key points of the proposal and as each screen came up the CEO said immediately 'read it'. At first Kevin assumed that he meant he had read it, but he realized that this was not the case. Kevin found he was getting more and more annoyed and was telling himself that this guy had no right to be so rude, nor did should he hold the position that he did with this lack of interpersonal skills.

It got to such a point that Kevin felt he was on the brink of leaving when he remembered something I had included in my book NLP at Work. He remembered that 'people make the best choices available to them at the time that they make them'. As this came to mind he considered that the way this CEO was behaving was the best he could do. Kevin might not like it, but that was the limit of the CEO's capability in this moment. The effect of this was that Kevin's anger disappeared. He relaxed and started to approach the presentation in the way in which he had originally intended. And something strange happened – the CEO started to respond and seemed to relax too. As the meeting progressed rapport between them built and, to use Kevin's words, 'we had a pretty good meeting'.

WHAT KINDS OF FILTERS ARE THERE?

MATCH/MISMATCH AND PAST/PRESENT/FUTURE

I have mentioned two filters – match and mismatch. There are probably thousands, maybe millions. Through learning how to model for yourself you can discover those filters that are unique to you and that make your experience what it is today, what it has been in the past and what you want it to be in the future. And here are some more filters – preference for thinking about past, present or future.

Where is your attention as you read this?

As you have been reading this chapter, you will have had thoughts about how what you are reading makes sense for you. Where did (do) you go to get these answers? Did you think back to moments in your experience or did you think about your life as it is today? Alternatively, did you think forward into the future to imagine how this would make sense then? Your choice is determined by your relative preferences for past, present or future. And this preference has implications for all aspects of your life, the decisions that you make, the way you behave at all times, the results that you achieve.

When you bought this book or when you chose to read it, what was your reason? Are you reading it to achieve something that you would really like in your work and in your life, and so want to move towards? Or are you reading it to change the way that things are for you? Are there problems or situations that you would rather not have, and so want to move away from? How have you spent your day so far? Thinking about how you would like it to be different and how you would like to change what you have? Or have you spent time thinking about what you would really like to achieve? (It may have been neither of these or it may have been both.) It is likely that your state will have varied quite considerably depending on which it was or how it shifted over time. If, for example, you have spent time thinking about problems, then it is possible that you feel somewhat low, maybe tense. Check your state right now – how does it feel? How are your neck, shoulders and muscles? Easy and relaxed or taut? This may give you some clues to the patterns in your thinking. If you are or have been thinking about how you really want things to be, you may be feeling inspired and self-motivated as you imagine what your future might look like.

The principle is that what you think is what you get. On this basis, if you can imagine how you want your life to be you increase the likelihood that it will be that way, not because the thinking alone makes it happen but because by thinking it you create a belief that it is possible. And what keeps someone going when nothing seems to go right is belief – belief that they can achieve what they really want.

Your choice in thinking will influence what you measure in performance. In your work, do your measures of performance concentrate on what you do want or what you don't? Do you measure problems or successes? Do you measure complaints or compliments? The difference in experience depending on your choice will be profound. Your choice will determine the content and tone of any review discussions. If they are problem based then you are inviting your meeting members to get into problem

TOWARDS/AWAY FROM

How are you feeling right now?

Do you measure problems or successes?

thinking states. If, on the other hand, they are success based, then your meeting participants will be concentrating on what has gone well and will be in the associated celebratory state. Which do you prefer? Which is most conducive to the business?

In Unipart they have 'blue sky meetings' where they explore what they really want to achieve in the future. Unipart has dramatically turned its business around from one that was dogged with problems to one that is famous as a model of success.

VISUAL/AUDITORY/ FEELING

'If you are or have been thinking about how you really want things to be, you may be feeling inspired and self-motivated as you imagine what your future might look like.' I quote this sentence from the previous page, where it may or may not have made sense to you. One of the factors that would have influenced this would be your preference for the sense that you use to take in information. If you take in information in a visual way, then to some extent this would have fitted you as the sense used to describe how you might imagine your future was visual – 'might look like'. If you prefer to absorb information in an auditory way, then you might have preferred me to say 'imagine what it might sound like'. You are more likely to prefer to hear these ideas rather than read them; it is likely that discussing them would be more suitable to your learning style. If, however, your preferred sense for taking in information is feelings, then you would probably rather be on a course where you can try these ideas out for yourself.

If in doubt, use all senses

So your degree of understanding and acceptance of what I am saying depends in part on the extent to which I can match the senses that you use to take in ideas. Difficult, huh? Especially when I don't know you. How can I know which sense to use? The answer is to use them all. This is true for anyone who wishes to appeal to a wide audience. If you use all styles – if your communication is enriched – then you will appeal to everyone in the way that you communicate. There is of course the little matter of content, but it has been shown in some forms of research that the method of our communication, as opposed to the content, is far and away the most influential element of what we do.

It's important to think big. It's wonderful if it comes off.

Simeone Nkoane

BIG CHUNK/ SMALL CHUNK

If you need facts to support abstract statements, then your preference is to require the detail – the small-chunk information. My preference is big chunk and consequently I am liable (if I don't think consciously about it) to give you generalized evidence without detailed facts to back it up (see the end of the previous paragraph!).

Have you ever been in a meeting where you wanted to get the broad picture, the general idea of what is happening, and someone else wants to pin down the details? Or conversely, have you ever wanted to find out exactly what is happening with some work that you have been promised, only to be fed some vague answers and approximate timeframes? Then again, have you been in a discussion with someone who just seems to dovetail with your approach and you swing along together without effort, sparking off ideas in each other? And have you ever been in a situation when you know that what is required of you needs a style that you don't find natural? In that situation, did you find someone who had a style different to your own and that you sometimes found challenging, but who nevertheless complemented you and together you established the balance needed to achieve the result?

Do you spark ideas off each other?

How we think about similarities and differences in style makes the difference in the way that we relate to and work with those around us. Big-chunk thinking can be ideal for strategic thinking. I once heard someone say that only 6 percent of the management population has the ability to think strategically. Small-chunk thinking suits planning and organizing. In business, as in life, we need both.

**ASSOCIATED/
DISSOCIATED**

How are you feeling about what I am saying? Are these words triggering feelings for you? Or are you taking what I am saying in a detached, analytical way? Do you get emotionally involved in what happens around you or do you tend to keep an emotional distance? When you attend meetings, do you engage emotionally with what is being discussed or do you sit back and keep some distance between yourself and what is happening? Do people think of you as being someone who shows and expresses their feelings, or are you someone who is known for your ability to keep a cool head when all is erupting around you?

We once had a representative from a major fire brigades on one of our courses. He commented that some of the fire crew experienced high levels of stress, to the extent that there was a high proportion of nervous breakdowns in the brigade. And he was also aware that some of the fire crew were able to manage their states much more effectively and healthily than others. This representative was responsible for personal development training and he was curious to know the 'difference that made the difference' between those who, even though they witnessed traumatic events, could put them aside and get on with their work and their life, and the others who seemed to relive the events and become increasingly traumatized by the memories.

There were many factors that made a difference, but one of the most significant was the ability on the part of the fire crew who had a healthy response to dissociate in their thinking from what had happened. They were also more likely to put the past to rest and to concentrate more on the present and the future. However, when there was a need to discuss or review the factors in any potentially disturbing incident, they thought about it in a dissociated way. They observed the situation as if they were outside of themselves and they heard it as if they were listening to themselves as an outsider. The effect of this choice in their thinking was that they remained emotionally detached and did not suffer the traumatic feelings of those who relived the situation as if they were there. These others saw it again as if they were seeing it through their own eyes, heard it through their own ears and consequently experienced the feelings over and over again.

What are you thinking as you read this chapter? Are you running through examples that connect with what I am saying? And if so, what kind of examples are you thinking of? Are you centered on what you are doing, have done or might do? Are you using incidents from your own experience or are you thinking how this affects others?

Bill was able to make connections with his own experience when he heard new ideas. This was one of the ways in which he managed his personal growth and learning. If he were in a group of people, he would often interrupt to give examples that related to him. Even when he was aware of this, he would apologize but still continue with his example. The way that he learned was by applying what he heard or saw to him.

When someone, perhaps your partner, tells you what sort of day they have had, do you respond by telling them about your own day or do you explore with them what they are saying?

Who do you put first, yourself or the other person?

Christine would invariably put others first. If there were a clash of priorities, she would automatically give way. If she were in a group with someone like Bill in the example above, she would let him interrupt and stop what she was saying. When he had finished, she would be most likely to ask him some more about what he had said.

The preference you hold will influence your relative sensitivity to yourself and others. For most business situations it would be desirable to have a balance between the two.

How have you thought about what has been covered in this chapter? Are you wondering about what you will do with what you have read? Maybe you have already come to some conclusions. Maybe you have some plans in place as to how you might use these ideas more than you do currently.

    Or are you thinking about how this affects the way in which you relate to those around you in work and in life?

Are you thinking about these ideas in terms of how they affect you and the people in your life?

Maybe you are considering particular events or a special occasion to which this thinking applies. Do you have a specific moment or time when you will apply what you have learned?

Possibly it is the ideas themselves that interest you. Maybe it is the topic of filters and language and thinking that is on your mind.

And then again perhaps you have particular places in mind. Are you recalling events by the places in which they occurred? Are you thinking about an environment in which you could use what you are reading?

How do you manage your time?

The choice you make determines how you use your time

The kind of choices you make will determine how you use your time and are a reflection of what is important to you in life. Is your life filled with activities or people? Or both? What matters to you? Is it objects or the subject of what you are involved with or is it the environment that matters? Are you thinking of taking a holiday this year and, if so, what are the deciding factors? Is it who you go with or the company of the people you expect to meet? Is it the place? Is the hotel or the venue that is important to you? Are you going on an activity holiday and is that what matters most? Is it the timing that is paramount or is it a celebration of a special occasion?

Your thinking affects how you make decisions about using your time. It also affects the kinds of memories, thoughts and imaginings you have and consequently the state that results from these.

Time management systems vs thinking styles

Many time management programs concentrate on what systems to use to organize your time. It will be your thinking style that will determine which of these you are most likely to use. Fundamentally, it is your thinking style that determines how you use your time in the first place.

GETTING INSIDE YOUR HEAD

Your thinking influences the style of your communication. If, for example, you think visually, you communicate with pictures either in your language or in the way you present. If you pay attention to what is different, it is likely that you will disagree or confront what others say to you. (You may not share this point of view, however!) If you filter for activity, you are likely to spend your time doing things. Similarly, you would be likely to want to know: 'What can I do with this?/What shall I do now?'

Your awareness of how you and others behave and communicate gives you access to the way that you and they think. Learning to recognize the characteristics is a means of modeling some of these internal processes so that you can get inside the head of the person you wish to model.

This awareness leads you to be able to answer the question: 'What has to be true for you/they to be doing what you/they are doing?'

Learning these filters is an aspect of modeling

Once upon a time there was a caterpillar who lived in a large tree in the park. Each day the caterpillar happily munched his way through the leaves of the tree, not really paying attention to very much else. On this one day, however, the caterpillar noticed something colorful fly around the top of the tree. He was dazzled by the bright orange and blue that caught the light of the sun and as this sparkling creature flew near the caterpillar could see that it was a beautiful butterfly. The butterfly seemed to float on the air as it brushed past the branch on which the caterpillar sat. 'Oh butterfly, how beautiful you are and how smoothly you fly – please show me how to fly like you.' The butterfly drifted close and smiled at the caterpillar. 'Be patient, little creature – one day, one day.' But the caterpillar was impatient and when the butterfly appeared again the next day, even more dazzling than before and circling the branches of the tree, the caterpillar asked once again: 'Please butterfly, teach me to fly like you.' The butterfly whispered low to the caterpillar: 'Be patient, one day you will.' The caterpillar was so frustrated that he decided to put the idea out of his mind altogether and eventually he forgot about his desire to fly.

Then one day something strange happened. It seemed as if the world had started to spin, one moment this way and the next moment that way. The caterpillar developed pains in his stomach and felt very ill. It seemed as if everything was blurred and distant. The world continued to spin, sometimes quickly, sometimes slowly. The caterpillar felt paralyzed and closed his eyes, thinking he must be dying. After a while, and he didn't know how long it had been, the world around seemed to settle and he felt lighter and free. He felt that he could move again and as he did he noticed the tree beneath him and he felt the warmth of the sun. In the distance he could hear a faint murmur and he felt himself drawn to the noise. It was a little voice speaking to him: 'Please will you show me how to fly the way you do.' 'Have patience – you will, you will.' Only then did he realize that he had become a butterfly.

THOUGHT PROVOKERS

1 Consider your job. How do you measure success – is it in terms of problems (even the reduction or absence of them) or is it in terms of what you really want to achieve?

2 Think of someone with whom you get on less well than you would like. What do you pay attention to – the extent to which they do meet your expectations or the extent to which they don't? What happens if you change what you pay attention to?

3 Think of a situation that occurred recently, which resulted in your feeling angry or frustrated in some way. What happened, but more to the point what meaning did you put on what happened? What did you do in the gap between the stimulus and the response that led to your feeling the way you did? Now think of a situation that also occurred recently that resulted in your feeling happy and good about the world. What happened here and how did you make sense of it? What did you in the gap?

4 How are you feeling right now? How are you filtering what is happening outside of yourself to create those feelings? How would you really like to be feeling and how can you make meaning out of your situation so that you can feel that way?

5 Think of someone with whom you get on well. What would you say are the dominant filters in their thinking and in the way that they behave and communicate? How do these compare with your own? Now think of someone with whom you don't get on so well. What do you think are the dominant filters in the way that they think and the way they communicate and behave? How do these compare with your own? Check out the similarities and differences with some more of your friends and colleagues and see if you can notice any patterns in what makes a difference with those who get on well and those who don't.

5   *The Subtleties of Thought*

Man is but a reed, the most feeble thing in nature; but he is a thinking reed ... All our dignity consists, then, in thought.

Blaise Pascal, *Pensées*, 1670

*I*N a *Sunday Times* article about the brilliance of Michael Schumacher on the eve of the 1997 Japanese Grand Prix, John Barnard, responsible for the technical development of the Arrows motor racing team, is quoted as saying:

It's a kind of mental attitude, a total commitment. He has this innate ability to go quickly, which means he is able to concentrate on what the car is doing a lot more. He can recount clearly every corner around the lap and this feedback is clear and sharp. It's what all the really good ones have got. Alain Prost was the same. You could talk about something a week after it had happened and he'd still give you the exact picture.

What John Barnard is referring to here is Michael Schumacher's ability to use his skill of visual recall and to do this with a precision that contributes significantly to his superior driving skill. He is showing an ability to detect, i.e. model, the crucial and yet often unconscious strategies that were contributing to Schumacher's success. With this kind of skill, managers and indeed anyone in business today could look at their top performers and identify the difference that makes the difference. Far from thinking of this difference as an innate skill, we can then think of it as something that can be learned and taught to others. Racing teams go to great lengths to conceal the secrets of their racing strategies and the latest technical developments that will give their cars the mechanical edge on the track. Yet some of the really key differentiators are the thinking strategies of the drivers. It is this magic ingredient that John Barnard has laid bare in his comments. One of the most priceless ingredients of success is available for all to see and use if they knew how.

A priceless ingredient

DISTINCTIONS IN THINKING PATTERNS

In NLP *at Work*, I explained how we have different modes of thinking and communicating, visual, auditory and feelings, and there was a discussion of these as filters in the previous chapter. When we remember images from our past, as Michael Schumacher clearly does, we are using our ability to recall **visually**. This is often accompanied by a look upwards and to our left. Consider for a moment some of the people you have dealt with this week and recall a time when you were with one of these people. Now recall what they were wearing. What color was their jacket or top? What style was their outfit and what kind of shoes were they wearing? Your skill in doing this or not is evidence of your familiarity with this way of thinking, i.e. visual recall, and your ability to do it.

Now think of something you have planned that you have not done before or think of someone you deal with but whose offices you have never visited.

Just this weekend I called in at the offices of our travel agents, based in Marlborough. All our dealings with them have been over the phone and each partner often refers to the other as being on another floor.

The street number of their offices is 142a. From all of this I had conjured up an image of a two-story apartment over the shops. I had imagined the premises to be quite plain, as I had assumed that most of their dealings with their clients were over the phone and that maybe appearances therefore weren't important to them. The reality was far from the truth. The premises are a delightful, almost exotic office opening on to the High Street – quite compact, but full of color and antique furniture.

I had used my ability to visually construct an image to create the scenario as I imagined it to be. In this case it was wrong, but that had no lasting detrimental impact on our working relationship. However, if I had the image of the premises as they actually are I might have been motivated to call in there before.

What we think affects our feelings and our anticipation of events and people. By choosing to think of these things as we want them to be, we influence not only our motivation towards the future but also our feelings in the present.

Think again about those people with whom you have been working this week. Can you recall what they were saying? Can you hear them as if they are speaking to you right now? This is your ability to **auditorily** recall sounds, which may be voices. My husband was recreating some files that had been damaged on my computer and he asked me what noise the computer made when loading systems in the past. He takes for granted his ability to recall sounds, although this is one of the key skills he accesses to solve problems on the systems with which he is working. And yet I would be surprised if there are many companies which specify this skill as one of the requirements for doing his kind of work, just as I doubt that anyone who is thinking of becoming a racing driver would ever imagine that their ability to visually recall the circuit with clarity is one of the essential ingredients for a champion.

We take for granted the skills that truly make a difference

This is another application of the modeling skill: the ability to detect the true qualities that make our top performers excel in the way that they do and to use those insights as the basis for the selection of more staff who can perform in the same way.

Can you imagine a sound that you have never heard before? Composers have the ability to imagine a musical score that is unique and different to what has gone before. Suppose that you want to influence one of your colleagues to respond to you in a way that they never have before. You may know someone who is usually hard sounding and sarcastic, but the response you would really like from them is a softer-sounding one – more compassionate. Imagine how that sounds. (This is your ability to use your auditory construct skill.) Have you done that?

Now imagine what you are saying to them that triggers this different response and how differently you sound when doing this. Imagine yourself speaking to them in a way that you never have before, in a tone of voice and a style that you have never used with anyone before. Most of NLP functions on the principle that what you think is what you get. If you want to get a particular response or if you want to be different in the future from what you have been in the past, whether that be in the way that you see, hear, sound or feel, then you first have to be able to imagine it.

First, imagine what you want

THE SUBTLETIES

I have often heard engineers say that they see problems in black and white. I have also seen skilled communicators talk and move with a regular rhythm. Some of the most inspiring leaders have the ability to engage the feelings of the people they influence by sharing their own passion in the way they interact with others. Each of these examples relies on a particular sense and a particular quality in the use of that sense; each mode of thinking has its own submodalities in the distinctions of how we use them. For example, when you look at a television screen you may be aware of the clarity of the picture, the sharpness of the color, the steadiness of the image. We have the same sorts of distinctions in the images on our internal television screens.

Some distinctions in the way we think visually include:

- whether the image is in black and white or color
- the sharpness of focus of the image or its haziness
- the nearness or distance of the picture
- whether we are in picture or outside of it looking at it as an observer
- the depth of the image (two- or three-dimensional)
- whether it is moving or still
- whether it is framed or panoramic
- the speed of movement in the image
- the number of images (like a split/multi-screen or not)
- the brightness or dullness
- the contrast of the picture
- the time it takes to come into focus
- whether it is changing or fixed
- the size of the image

The distinctions in the way we think in an auditory way include:

- volume
- speed of sound
- clarity or dullness of what we hear
- location of the sound
- whether it is in stereo or mono
- tone of the sound
- whether it is a sound or voices
- a rhythm or not
- the duration of the sound
- the extent to which it is continuous or discontinuous

And the distinctions in the way we experience feelings include:

- the location in our body of the feeling
- the intensity of the feeling
- the quality of the feeling, i.e. sharp, prickly, throbbing
- the duration of the feeling
- the pattern it follows or its steadiness
- texture – rough or smooth

- weight
- shape
- size
- temperature

SO WHAT?

Our memories, our present experience, our expectations for our future and our goals are made up of combinations and sequences of these thinking distinctions. Our memories and the way we hold them in our thinking, the meaning we put to experiences and events in everyday life and work and our imaginings are what make our life what it is.

On this basis, everything we experience on the outside is a mirror to the way we form our perceptions on the inside. Do you wonder what is outside of your experience? Something might be just in front of you but you cannot see it because you don't have the representation of it within.

What we experience is a mirror to our internal perceptions

There is a story in *The Fifth Discipline Fieldbook* of a ewe who disowns her lamb immediately after birth, believing it not to be her own, and wanders the farm bleating and looking frantically for the 'lost lamb', while all the time the very lamb is scurrying behind her, desperately trying to feed from its mother.

So by developing our awareness of the way we represent our world, we begin to discover how we shape our experience to be what it is. And by implication, through this awareness we begin to have the choice to make our experience more of what we really want it to be.

We can only influence our situations from the inside – we have no control over what happens on the outside of ourselves – and managing these distinctions in our thinking is part of the way we do this. Imagine what it might be like to have only the sweet smell of success in your nostrils or to view the world through rose-colored glasses and to hear the winds of change. Perhaps you can develop a taste of what is to come and warmly congratulate yourself on what you have done with your life

We influence from within

to date. These examples might not quite ring true for you, so choose how you would like it to be for you in a way that fits with the significant people in your life as well as for yourself. You can create a representation of a life and a business that fit for you and the criteria that are important to you; one that fits with your values and your beliefs and sits comfortably with the kind of person that you are. All this being the case, you will be on course to fulfill any higher purpose for what you do and what you want to achieve.

THE SWISH

Self-awareness is the foundation for coaching

Being aware of the way in which you represent your memories, your present experience and your future in itself gives you choice. Building awareness of what is forms the foundation for coaching yourself and others into new choices. There will be one or two key distinctions in your thinking that create the meaning that you make of what happens to you. It may be, for example, that your pleasant memories are brighter and closer, whereas the less pleasant ones are dark and further away. There is an exercise at the end of this chapter that will help you to check this out. Or perhaps the sharpness of the voice with which you talk to yourself for those experiences you consider to be failures is in contrast with the softer, slower tones you use for those moments you experience as successes.

The SWISH is a technique for changing these distinctions so that you can transform a response you would rather not make into one you would. It works best on visual representations, although it can be used on others.

It is one thing to be aware of your patterns in thought and the impact that they have on your responses to situations and to people. It is quite another to change them. Our habitual ways of thinking become grooved in. For example, people in your life will trigger particular responses. Certain events, sounds, visual images or even a smell, a taste or a touch will trigger a certain response. Who are the people in your life who spark a tingle of pleasure in you when you see them? And are there any people at whose appearance you feel yourself tense up? Maybe there is that certain tone of voice that causes you to tell yourself to watch out, or conversely the mellow undertones of another person that create a warm sensation throughout your body.

Nicholas Brealey, my publisher, knows when he has a good book in front of him when the hairs on the back of his neck start to rise (he would emphasize that this is not the only criterion!). We each have our own unique set of responses to external and internal stimuli. The question is whether they are the responses you want. Suppose that each time you see your boss you imagine yourself small and them large by comparison, resulting in your feeling and acting in a subservient way. Or possibly each time you are faced with an important meeting, the moment you see the open door and the faces of the other people inside you start to tell yourself what is wrong with your proposal. These sorts of responses are unlikely to work in favor of your business goals. They can nevertheless be so habitual that you are unaware of them, so much so that you blame the external stimulus for the feelings that you have. The truth is that it is you and what you do with those stimuli that create the response within yourself.

The SWISH is named after the noise you can make to reinforce the change that you want to make for yourself. It is designed to replace less useful responses with ones that are more in line with the way that you really want to be. It is a simple exercise that works with the patterns in the way you think. It enables you to make new connections between the resources you have and the outcomes you want to achieve.

THE SWISH

---

1   First, identify the response in yourself that you want to change. What exactly is the reaction that you would like to replace?

2   Identify what it is precisely that triggers this response. There will be some specific that immediately precedes your reaction. Identifying this trigger is a key part of the process. If, for example, it is a response to the way that someone speaks to you, identify what it is that they say or what it is about the way that they say it that triggers your reaction. Recreate this in your thinking in exactly the way that it happens. If it is the way that someone speaks to you, then hear them saying the words that they say in exactly the way that they do. If it is the sight of an audience in front of you, imagine yourself in that situation looking out at the audience in the way that you do. See exactly what you see as if you were there.

3   Now determine which facets of the way that you think about this trigger have the greatest effect. There will be some elements that intensify your reaction. The SWISH lends itself most readily to visual triggers and most often the size and brightness of the image have the greatest impact. For example, if it is the sight of a certain person who works for you that triggers a response, then experiment with what happens when you make your image of them bigger first of all and then brighter. Experiment with each distinction in turn, putting the image back the way it was before you experiment with the next one. The aim is to find the one or two that intensify your response. Although these elements are currently triggering the response that you don't want, the aim of the SWISH is to hook these elements to the response that you do want. In so doing, you are making your own resources work for you rather than against you. This way of effecting change really does draw on

the fact that we have all the resources we need to achieve what we want. The challenge is how to rechannel them.

4   Think about something completely different to 'break your state'. For example, what color was the front door of the house that you last lived in?

5   Now imagine the person that you would like to be irrespective of what you have been in the past and irrespective of any specific behavior. This is an opportunity to imagine how you would like to be, the sort of qualities that you would really like to have, the style that really fits with who you truly are. Imagine yourself being who you know you truly are and really want to be. Imagine this as if you are looking at yourself as an observer, dissociated. Develop this until you have an image that is compelling and truly desirable. Check that this 'you' really fits for the significant people in your life – it needs to be a real benefit to them too for you to be this new way. Explore how this fits with whatever sense of purpose you have, with your beliefs and values – with every aspect that is important to you. Check that this 'new you' meets any needs that you may have been satisfying in less healthy ways in the past. If, for example, you have been getting attention for being stressed, check that you are going to get the level and quality of attention that you need from this new way of being in the world.

6   Think of something completely different. For example, what is your telephone number backwards?

7   Make an image of the trigger, the stimulus that prompts the response that you want to change. Use the key factors that enhance the trigger, e.g. if the distinctions of size and brightness intensify the trigger, then make this image bright and big.

8   Take the image of the 'new you' and make it small and dark. Place this small, dark image in the corner of the bigger image.

9   Very quickly make the large image small and dark and **at the same time** make the small image large and bright. Do this as fast as you can – the speed is important. You can make a sound to accompany this movement – a SWISH sound, hence the name. But you can choose any other sound that fits for you provided it is one that enhances the speed of the change. The sound can become the association for the feelings of becoming this new you. Break state. Clear the images so that you start afresh. Create a new image so that you break the sequence before you start again. Without doing this, you may find that you have set it up to loop around rather than working in the direction that you desire, i.e. from the trigger problem state to the new you.

10 Repeat the process five times and check to see if it works. You will know this if when you either experience or imagine the trigger situation your response to it has changed and you SWISH into the new you automatically. If this is not happening, go back and experiment with some other elements of the process to find the 'difference that makes the difference'.

We do this sort of thinking automatically, although sometimes we may misdirect our efforts. I was with a manager recently when they were told they had to go to New York at short notice on a business trip. They SWISHED themselves into an unresourceful state in a matter of seconds and, instead of anticipating this long-awaited trip with pleasure, they were preparing for it with dread! They had the structure of the SWISH but they were using it in the wrong direction. Once we understand how we do what we do, then we have choices as to how to use the skills that we already have in more constructive and healthy ways. We do have all the resources we need – we sometimes just need to learn how to use them more appropriately.

●●●

There is a story about a wolf who learned how to dig up traps and turn them over. He evidently enjoyed this procedure because he did it often. One day a trapper inadvertently buried a trap upside down, and when the wolf came and turned it over he caught himself. He was smart enough to dig up traps, but not smart enough to leave them alone.

THOUGHT PROVOKERS

1   Identify two memories – one 'good', one less 'good'.
    Consider each of the thinking distinctions in turn –
    visual, auditory and feeling – and note how you
    represent each memory. What is the same and what is
    different? If you wish to change the less 'good' memory
    into a 'good' one, use either the SWISH technique (on
    page 72) or take the distinctions that are different for the
    two memories and one at a time apply the distinctions
    of the 'good' memory to the less 'good' one. Be sure to
    put your representation back to what it was between
    each change you make in order to isolate the ones that
    make the biggest difference in your response.

2   Think of something that you do well – a skill that you use
    in your work or a result that you know you can achieve
    consistently well. Ask yourself how you do this. Explore
    the distinctions of how precisely you do each element
    until you have the specifics of how you think about what
    you do. You will undoubtedly find that there are ways of
    thinking that you do unconsciously and subsequently take
    for granted that are key components in your success.

3   Identify a skill or a quality that you admire in someone
    else. Get yourself into a position where you can observe
    them using this skill. This need not be with you, in fact it
    can be easier if you are watching and listening to them
    using the skill with someone else. Listen to their words.
    What distinctions in thinking patterns do they indicate
    with the words they use? Watch the movements they
    make, especially their eye movements. Which senses are
    they accessing as they proceed? These sorts of clues
    relay far more valuable information than anything the
    person may tell you. The patterns in thinking that make
    the difference are often taken for granted by the subject
    and are often so fleeting that they are not consciously
    aware of them. You will have been successful in
    identifying not only the distinctions in thinking patterns but
    also the sequence in which the person uses them.

Language and Metaphor 6

A modern poet tells how once the doer of an heroic deed was unable to tell it to his fellow-tribesmen for lack of words. Whereupon there arose a man 'afflicted with the necessary magic of words', and he told the story in terms so vivid and so moving that 'the words became alive and walked up and down in the hearts of his hearers'.

William Barclay

WORDS used well delight me. I choose books that are admired for the author's skill with words and the quality of the writing, ones that attract testimonials such as these:

Roy writes ... with a fecund, teeming visuality that is entirely her own. A masterpiece, utterly exceptional.

William Dalrymple review of Arundhati Roy's
The God of Small Things

I can't imagine any writer reading it without complete admiration, and a kind of gratitude, because if a book like that can be written in a culture like this, it's terrific for all of us.

Michael Hers review of *Underworld* by Don DeLillo

This book is an aria and a wolf whistle of our half-century. It contains multitudes.

Michael OnDaatje review also of *Underworld*

It will come as no surprise that a third of NLP, the *l* in neuro-linguistic programming, is to do with language. We have moved from a business culture dependent on our ability to manufacture goods to one that centers on our ability to offer services and meet customer needs. This requires a particular skill with words and behavior. It requires an ability to manage ourselves in a way that we have never needed before.

Journey through the North Pole!

'Through' and not 'at'

Paul Kiss, one of the participants on our Personal Mastery course had always secretly held the goal of being a part of an expedition that journeyed to the magnetic North Pole. He is also the managing director of a building firm, Abbey Pynford, so it wasn't as if he had lots of time to create this possibility. What he discovered during his personal development was that the goal as he had thought about it to date was outside of his control – he could not make an expedition choose him. However, what he could control was his ability to make himself eligible and desirable to be selected to join an expedition. And he was. And he got there.

He used all the skills and thinking he had learned to manage himself in the process. He returned so inspired by his experience that he set up a project to give this same confidence and motivation to achieve the seemingly impossible to schoolchildren of all ages. However, he tells of other people on the expedition with him who have been depressed since their return from the North Pole, with a lack of motivation to do anything else now that their life's goal has been achieved. Their goals stopped at the point at which they reached the North Pole. His thinking included reaching the North Pole, but went way beyond it. His thinking was 'through' and not 'at'. And what of his business, you might ask, while all of this is going on? It has surpassed all targets and he is spending less time directly involved and more time leading and coaching.

THE MAP IS NOT THE TERRITORY

I came upon the words 'the map is not the territory' in the early days of my NLP learning. We each have our own unique map of the world, our own inner domain. If we wish to understand each other and how and why we do what we do, then first we need to accept this premise. Modeling is the exploration of this inner territory.

Your inner world is unique

If I want to understand how you do what you do, I need first of all to accept that your inner world is unique to you. There may be similarities between your inner world and my own, but it is very unlikely that the specifics will be the same. And yet we take so much of this inner world for granted. When I did my early NLP training I was shocked to discover that not everyone was consciously aware of the images they hold in their head. This is how I think predominantly and I had often invited participants on my training to visualize what they were going to do. No one had said that they couldn't do this, although I recognize now that we just accept instructions, even those that make little sense, and adapt them to fit our own internal world.

So our experience of the world is a metaphor. To take on the way that someone else does what they do, I need to be able to live in their metaphor.

DIFFERENT LANGUAGE

I was having a discussion with my husband about the different styles that we and others use in conversation. We started to compare our respective styles and the way we had reacted to each other throughout the day. He had frequently mismatched the points I had made, for example when I had commented on how quiet the roads were and how often this was the case on that route, he had disagreed and pointed out that they hadn't been quiet the last time we had made this journey. I had said throughout the day how I was feeling and I now explained how I felt as a result of his (seemingly constant) mismatching, which was that I felt he wasn't listening to me and that he was not only discounting my points but me too. He was astonished, but also told me how frustrated he was when I remarked on how I felt, particularly if this was an implied or actual negative that I attributed to his disagreements.

I could feel our emotions becoming increasingly engaged in what we were saying. We were reliving the feelings we were describing. He explained that when he 'disagreed' with a point I made, in his thinking he was adding a fact that made the overall picture of what we were discussing broader. But when I made comments about how I felt as a result of what he was saying, he found that distressing because he saw nothing he could do about it.

What this conversation highlighted for me was the unique representation that we each have of the world, which can be expressed in the language we use. For all the training I have done, it is so easy for me to assume that the way in which I perceive the world and the everyday situations within it is the same for others. Of course I know this is not the case, but I am always realizing it afresh. And so often the profound realizations come when I am prepared to push through the emotions that engage when I touch on something I experience as sensitive.

Realizations come when we push through our emotions

If I want to have the same skill as my husband, the skill of enjoying what I would call an argument, then I need to be able to take on his map of the world. There was a time when I truly did not have this skill – when I would avoid arguments like the plague and feel personally offended and hurt if someone on one of my courses disagreed with me – but I have it now. I can accept and learn from those times when a participant disagrees with me and I usually enjoy it when they do, but I can also accept that there is so much more I can do to enjoy this skill in everyday situations. On balance I still prefer harmony to conflict, acceptance to dispute. And so my husband offers me a way of experiencing disagreement that will make it perfectly OK for others to have a different point of view to my own.

To do this, I first needed to find out in more detail just how he experienced discussions and then take that strategy on board for myself. If as a result I experience disagreements as additional points of view that make the overall picture broader, then it has worked. So one of the benefits is that I have acquired new ways of thinking that increase my flexibility and therefore my choices when I want to achieve a result.

In a different frame, when I understand how someone else is experiencing a situation, in this case what I have previously referred to as an argument, then I come closer to being in deeper rapport with them. When I have this rapport I learn how to talk to them, how to present my ideas and how to listen to them in a way that they accept and understand, instead of expecting them to adjust the way that I think and communicate to fit for them. Let's face it, who would you rather do business with, who would you rather be with, who would you rather listen to – someone who respects the way in which you like to do business and the way you process your ideas and thoughts, or someone who expects you to do the translating?

Who would you rather do business with?

METAPHOR FOR MODELING

The clues to our inner world abound. Take some of the sentences in the previous section:

- 'What this conversation highlighted for me...'
- 'Profound realizations come when I am prepared to push through the emotions.'
- '...when I touch on something I experience as sensitive.'
- 'He was adding a fact that made the overall picture of what we discussing broader.'

These references to the senses contain clues to how we are thinking at the time that we say them. And they are still only clues, because you cannot know exactly what I mean when I talk of pushing through emotions, or what I am seeing, hearing and feeling when I do this. Even I don't consciously know until I explore what happens in my experience when I do this.

Some say that the eyes are the windows to the soul. I believe that our language is a doorway to our inner world, the world of imagery, sound and emotion. By developing our skill in what is said and what is not said, what is meant consciously and what is meant unconsciously, we build our ability to model through metaphor.

At the heart of the process of modeling is the question....

What has to be true for someone to be saying this?

COME TO YOUR SENSES

In the examples above, the words 'highlighted' and 'picture' indicate that I am thinking visually, just as the words 'push' and 'touch' point towards the fact that I am engaging feelings, either physiological or emotional. Not surprisingly, this snapshot of thoughts reveals my two preferred senses in the way that I think. By paying attention to what happens in a moment, we have an insight into how we live our lives. What I see and how my environment looks are important to me. What I notice engages my feelings and I make decisions based on what I see.

Every moment encapsulates our approach to life

Recently we were interviewing for one of our office jobs and I was influenced by how the applicants parked their cars outside our offices. I was influenced by how they looked and how they made eye contact or not when we met. My feelings towards them were filtered through these senses. Being aware of this, I can plan to assess them with other objective means, but there are undoubtedly other subjective evaluations that come into play.

One of my associates who is sensitive to the way in which I think and make decisions sends me faxes with his ideas set out before seeing and talking to me, either face to face or on the phone. Some people might think this is manipulative; I think it is sensitive and respectful. And this again illustrates how we use metaphor as a way of making meanings that work for us.

In contrast, if I were thinking in an auditory way I might tell you what I want to hear and how your idea sounds to me. I might describe what I had heard in a discussion.

In NLP *at Work*, there is a detailed chapter on the characteristics of thinking and communicating with each of the different senses. Some more examples of the patterns in language that are characteristic of each of the senses are as follows:

VISUAL

- visible means of support
- a glimpse of reality
- I was exposed to
- she saw me through it
- we face a new challenge
- the brilliant sky
- we looked after our interests
- new way of seeing the world

AUDITORY

- I have cited in the text
- he wasn't mentioned
- the important question we are all asking is...
- she argued that...
- we spoke on the phone
- the answers that are demanded
- so you say
- I heard it from his own lips

FEELINGS

- driving an organization
- hopes and frustrations
- the birth pangs
- we reshaped the work
- a sting in the tail
- crisply formulated
- it hit home
- executive burnout
- stress levels
- a period of relaxation
- moving through

These expressions give us some ideas as to what senses are in play at the time they are used, but even then some can be ambiguous. As a rule do not assume – check out in as many ways as you can what sense is being accessed if the precision of the strategy is important to you.

MAKING MEANINGS

In language we distort, generalize and delete. Our spoken words are a metaphor for our inner world, which is in turn a metaphor for our experience. When you meet or talk to someone, you make meanings of those aspects that are important to you.

In the interviews I mentioned above, one of my colleagues came to different conclusions to me. She admired the skills that one woman had described and had talked with her at length about how she could contribute to the business. My colleague had deleted some of the information to which I was paying attention, and vice versa.

Different people make different meanings of the same conversation. We each distort what we hear and what we see and feel to fit into our respective inner experience. Making meanings that fit for us is a way of distorting what happens in our external world. Some of the meanings that we make work for us; others don't work or lead to feelings of unresourcefulness.

Some meanings work for us and some don't

Suppose that someone close to you frequently points out mistakes that you have made. You could choose to believe that they want you to feel down and unresourceful. Alternatively, you could choose to believe that they must care about you a great deal to give you so much of their attention. The meaning that you make is within your control and the choice that you make determines your emotional state. What would you rather have – an emotional state that works for you or one that works against you?

GETTING AT THE UNSAID

So how can you explore the inner experience of the person you wish to model? Questions are one way of getting behind the words.

To question someone to elicit how they are thinking, you need to be neutral in the way you ask the questions. If, for example, you ask someone how they *felt* when they started their presentation, then you are steering them to tell you about their *feelings*. If you don't use that kind of prompt you will get their intuitive and most natural response, which is what you want. When you model you want to know exactly what is going on for them, so your questions need to be as neutral and as invisible as possible.

Here are some examples:

- Tell me how you go about...
- What happens next?
- And then?
- Can you say some more?
- What is important to you at this point?
- How do you know?
- How do you do that?
- What makes a difference?
- What is going on for you as this is happening?
- So you [summarize what they have told you] and then ...?

However, be aware that the questions themselves are an influence. As in physics, it is impossible to observe without influencing the process in some way. So the ultimate test lies in the implementation of the strategy. If having modeled a strategy, you use it and it works, then you have what you wanted. And if when you teach this to others they can also achieve the result, then the modeling has been successful. And if the person that you originally modeled can also use this strategy with greater consistency knowing the structure of what they do, then it has been even more successful. If it works it's NLP!

If it works it's NLP!

A couple were having problems in the way that they were relating to each other in the marriage. They went for counseling individually. The husband confessed to the counselor: 'I just don't love her any more.' 'So just love her,' the counselor replied.

THOUGHT PROVOKERS

1 What metaphor would you (do you) use to think about:
   a) your work?
   b) your life?
   c) your relationships?
2 What is the upside of each metaphor? For example, if you think of life as a bed of roses, then it is sweet smelling and colorful.
3 What is the downside of each metaphor? For example, roses have thorns.
4 Reread something that you have written. What is the balance in your use of visual, auditory, feelings and neutral language?

Levels of Change 7

In spite of all our hopes, dreams, and efforts, change is real and
forever. Accept it fearlessly. Investigate the unknown; neither fear nor
worship it.

Joseph A Bauer, Love Me Tender, Love Me True

So many of the applications of NLP in the business
world have been to do with how to build rapport,
whether that be face to face, over the phone or in writing. I
would say that the ability to build relationships through
your skill in building rapport is one of NLP's best
contributions to the business world. To build rapport with
others, you need first of all to be in rapport with yourself.
What you give others comes from within yourself.

*What you give others comes
from within yourself*

*I remember witnessing a presenter of NLP do a very interesting
session on the importance of rapport in my early NLP training. I was
impressed and could see the relevance and application to most if not all
business and everyday situations. Imagine my surprise when,
following in this same trainer's path to the refreshments room, I saw
him more or less elbow his way through the coffee queue to get served
first!*

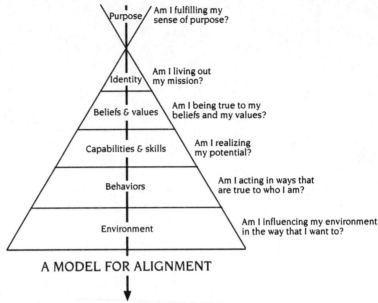

A MODEL FOR ALIGNMENT

When all of these elements line up with each other,
you have alignment – a rapport with yourself

Figure 3   The logical levels of change model

The logical levels of change model (Figure 3) was first developed and presented by Gregory Bateson, anthropologist and author of *Towards an Ecology of Mind*, and subsequently enhanced by Robert Dilts, one of the most innovative developers of the applications of NLP in the world today. The model lends itself to many applications, including allowing you to explore to what extent you are in rapport with yourself:

- Are you doing work that is in line with what you believe to be important?
- Are you taking actions day by day to further your purpose in life?
- Are you consistently true to yourself in what you do and what you say and how you do that?
- Are you realizing your true potential in the way that you are using your core talents and skills?
- Do your surroundings communicate messages about

yourself that you feel are an accurate expression of who you are and what you stand for?

- Do you rest easy at night knowing that you have acted and thought in ways of which you are proud?
- Do you feel that your heart and mind are at one?

Are your heart and mind at one?

If the answer to all of these questions is yes, then you are truly in rapport with yourself.

SEVERAL LEVELS OF THINKING AND FEELING

Change, state, learning and performance are influenced by several levels of thinking and feeling. If you only study what you or someone else is doing then you may have missed a key piece, their belief in what is possible.

My husband often plays squash or racket ball. His technique is good and he is willing to share some of his tactics for playing well, e.g. where to position yourself on the court, how to move your body and how to make certain strokes. However, if that were all you studied and put into practice, you would be missing what I believe is one of the most important aspects of his game – his belief in how he is going to play. With hardly an exception, he is convinced that he is going to win. The result of holding this belief is that he usually wins against people who are more technically skilled and generally fitter than he is. He often wins against people who are much younger than him, who have sometimes said that they will show him what a fit youngster will do!

I have sometimes shared this example on courses I run and people have asked whether he feels devastated if he loses. The answer is no, not at all. He very definitely lives out the presupposition that there is no failure, only feedback, and he uses the experience to set his course of action for the next time.

This example illustrates the point that it is not one isolated element that makes the difference. It is a combination of tactics, beliefs and skills that results in the performance you experience. Often there are just one or two elements that really are the difference that makes the difference. The goal of modeling is to find out what they are and reproduce them.

So let's look at each level of change in detail.

ENVIRONMENT

Chapter 8, Environmental metamessages, goes into one aspect of this in depth, on the assumption that our environment is an expression of who we are, what we believe and value and how we think. How you organize your environment and what you decide to do or even not to do with it is an expression of what is going on inside of you.

I sit and write looking out over a valley in one of the most rural parts of the Dordogne in Southwest France. I cannot quite see the horizon as it is shrouded in a New Year mist. My fingers are a bit stiff as we only arrived in France yesterday and the house is still a bit cold, although there is a log-burning stove glowing behind me. My husband is keeping the stove stocked with a supply of dry wood from the barn, which is attached to the house. We are nearly a mile away from our nearest neighbors and although I organize it so that the phone does not ring and disturb us here, I can communicate via e-mail and fax. We have the latest technology unobtrusively to hand to access the resources we need to do whatever work we want.

This environment is an expression of who I am. There are aspects of this that I am consciously aware of, just as there will be things that you read into this environment of which I am unaware but nevertheless say something about both you and me! You can learn things about me just as I can learn about myself from how I organize myself here. I have an array of book chapters spread neatly down the table to my right and I have a schedule of chapters to write and contacts to make laid out in front of me. Everything communicates what I am thinking and how I am organized within myself. So a study of how someone exists within their environment will often tell you things that they would not be able or even consider putting into words.

I also use environment to refer to anything we put outside of ourselves in our thinking and experience. For example, a salesperson who says 'It's tough out there' referring to the customers they are dealing with is putting their experience outside of themselves. Anyone who refers to 'the management' or 'they' as being the source of their experience is attributing what is happening to them as being outside of themselves. I find the use of language in this respect invaluable in terms of finding out how someone experiences the factors that influence the results they get. Is the source within them or is it outside?

To model at the level of environment, pay attention to the person's physical manifestations – to whatever is outside of them in practical and linguistic terms. What do you notice in their surroundings? How do they dress? What do they put outside of themselves in their language? Look for patterns, which you can then check out at the other levels. You may not know what these patterns or observations mean – it is enough initially to be aware of them.

BEHAVIOR: WHOLE BODY LISTENING

In Chapter 15, High-performance Coaching, I talk about someone who omitted to refer to themselves in conversation. They did not use 'I'. Even when they were alluding (and alluding is how they did this) to their own thoughts or feelings, they managed to delete 'I' from the sentence. To notice this is to model. At the time I was talking to someone who had lost their personal confidence and self-esteem.

Modeling behavior means paying attention to what we are saying and what we are doing and how we are doing these things. The more sensitive you are in what you pay attention to, the more sophisticated will be your modeling skills. For example, do you notice where someone looks each time you ask them a question? Do you know how you indicate past, present and future in the way you map out space around you?

People speak with their
gestures

I was in conversation with someone recently and as they referred to their past they always referred to a point two years before and simultaneously gestured to their right. As they referred to the future, they gestured to their left and they clearly had the intervening times spaced evenly between the two. Knowing this helped me to know where in time they were even when they didn't include the details in their words. They told me with their gestures.

When you pay attention to the patterns that people reveal with their movements and gestures, you gain an insight into what their unconscious mind is telling you, of which their conscious mind may be unaware.

This attention to body language is so different from the interpretations that you will get if you read something with a title like 'How to read a person like a book'. These sorts of books say things like if someone has their arms crossed then they are being defensive. If someone touches their nose with the back of their hand then they are telling lies. It can be valuable to be aware of some of the generalized meanings – as long as you realize that this is all they are. And this is *not* what sensitivity to body language in the context of NLP is about.

Being truly sensitive to your own and others' body language means recognizing the unique patterns that we each use to communicate what we really mean. It is your ability to calibrate to these unique patterns that matters in modeling. To reproduce the results that someone else gets, you need in part to replicate their behavior. The more precision you use in the way that you do this, the more accuracy you will get in reproducing the results that they achieve.

Can you be aware of the following?

- The patterns in someone's gestures as they talk to you or as they listen.
- Their eye movements as they talk or as they think.
- How they gesture to indicate time.
- The difference in posture when they are talking about

something they have done well compared with
something they have not.

- When and how their complexion changes color.
- What patterns they use in their language.
- What is deleted from their language.
- What is distorted in their language.
- What is generalized in their language.
- How their tone of voice changes and when they do this.
- Any different patterns of behavior and when they use
  each pattern.
- How they move and walk.
- How their muscles tense and relax.
- How their breathing changes and when this happens.

These are some examples of things that you need to be
aware of at the level of behavior. It is the ability to read
what is happening that enables you to listen with the
whole of your body to the whole of theirs.

One of my work team sometimes finds difficulty in
saying when they feel concerned about something that has
been said to them. On the surface they will joke and smile.
The real communication comes from their skin tone.
Although their face remains the same color, when they feel
upset their neck goes red in one small section beneath
their ear. If you did not pay close attention you would not
notice this, but if you have the sensitivity and awareness
of a good modeler you would. You might not know at first
what it means, but if you pay attention over time you can
connect this specific behavioral response to specific kinds
of occasions.

CAPABILITIES

A new term has entered our vocabulary in the last few
years: emotional intelligence. And this is in contrast to
intellectual intelligence. Emotional intelligence is
concerned with the skills we bring to bear on everyday
situations, it is not to do with what qualifications or
experience we have. It may have led to us getting certain

*Emotional intelligence vs
intellectual intelligence*

qualifications and it will for sure have been instrumental in what we made of our experience, but it is related to what talents we have and demonstrate in what we do moment by moment, day by day.

I recently had a discussion with someone who couldn't believe that any employer would be brave enough to take someone on for the skills they demonstrated as opposed to the qualifications they had on paper or the years of experience they could prove they had. My reaction to this is that I find it difficult to imagine how anyone could be stupid enough not to learn to evaluate and assess the skills of the present as opposed to the words of the past!

One of our best friends is the international IT infrastructure manager for one of the largest consultancies in the world. He left school at the age of 15 without any GCSEs and to this day has no paper qualifications, and yet he is one of the most sought-after people in his profession.

Your capabilities are the inherent skills that you use to achieve the results that you do. Sometimes we find that we have capabilities that may be misused, but they are nevertheless skills that could bring about different results when transferred to other areas of our lives. For example, if you have the capability to sulk for hours, then you have the capability of holding one emotional state over a period of time. What if you could use that same capability to hold a state of motivation or confidence for at least the same period of time? We all have excellence within us – it is just that it is not always used to best advantage.

In my eldest son James's last year at school I was asked to go in to see one of his teachers, as there was a problem and the teacher wanted to speak to me about the punishment. Apparently James had not booked himself on to a visit to one of the universities as part of the maths course. This visit was meant to give the pupils a taste of what maths lectures at university were like. When James discovered that his friends had booked on to the trip he was disappointed, as the main motivation for him at the time was to stay in the company of his mates. So without telling the teachers, he got himself down to Southampton where the lectures were being held and into the lectures, but without permission.

I understand the implications of his not letting people know where he was, but it seemed to me that the teacher's reaction to this was one of indignation that James was not doing what he was told. What amused me was the lack of appreciation of James's tenacity and motivation to get himself independently to where he wanted to be. To me these are skills to be valued in other contexts and the recognition and use of these on the part of the teacher would have been far and away the most successful strategy to get an all-round win–win outcome for the school and for James. This teacher was not open to this way of thinking, with the result that James lost all interest in maths and decided to take another subject at university instead.

By recognizing all our talents and capabilities, we use the energy that exists in a situation to achieve a result that fits for everyone. But first we need to know what those capabilities are. The question at the heart of NLP modeling is: 'How do you/they/he/she/I do that?' You can apply this to anything that you or others do, 'good' or 'bad'.

How do you do that?

You could ask 'How do they do that?' of someone who:

- makes you feel good whenever you see them
- regularly gets depressed
- brings energy into any group or team they work with
- consistently feels anger towards others
- recognizes the beauty in others no matter who they are
- can play on words in such a way that they bring an amusing twist to everyday conversations
- can be gracious and giving no matter what company they are in
- sees only the problems and the bad news in the world
- looks at a page of computer code and immediately sees the bugs
- can go into a shop and not make a decision to buy what they want
- feels stressed when others have expectations of them

You have a raft of talents

Behind everything that you and the people in your life do is a raft of talents. Some of these talents you will be using in ways that enrich your own and others' lives; there will be others that could be redirected but are currently channeled towards less productive ends.

BELIEFS AND VALUES

Our beliefs and our values are a part of the fabric that makes us who we are. What we hold to be true about ourselves and what is deep-down important to us are at the heart of who we are as people. So in a way it still surprises me how much we reveal of these core pieces in the everyday things that we say and do. And so often people tell you their core beliefs: they lay them out on the table of life for all to see who choose to see them.

Beliefs are not facts

What you believe to be true is not a fact, it is an emotionally held opinion. You may have inherited it or you may have learned it or you may have been given it by your parents or your teachers or similar figures in your lives. What did your parents teach to believe about yourself and how do you live that belief out in your life today? We tend to live our lives in a way that is designed to prove our beliefs to ourselves. One thing is sure – you believe that you are right (in your world) and you will do whatever you can, consciously and unconsciously, to prove this is the case.

Gordon is a tall, good-looking young man who has had a number of opportunities to develop his career and his life. At first he does well and he often feels euphoric with the results he achieves. However, each event takes a similar turn. Whenever he gets close to being recognized by others for what he is doing and is within reach of achieving a position of some relative security, something seems to go wrong. It is as though he sabotages the imminent success when he is within inches of its realization. When he talks about his upbringing he will tell you that his father never realized his ambitions and never fully used the talents he had. Gordon has learned to live in his father's footsteps. He has learned to hold the same beliefs about himself that his father had. And what they both learned is not a fact but an emotionally held belief that they cannot ultimately succeed.

Your beliefs determine your capabilities, which in turn drive your behavior, which leads to the results that you get, and which influences events and people around you.

Beliefs determine capabilities

To discover someone's beliefs you can do any of the following:

- Listen to them and they will usually tell you: 'I'm no good at making friends.' 'I always fall on my feet.' 'I think everyone in this world has the right to be loved.' 'You can't trust anyone in business today.' 'What you give is what you get.' 'The response I get from others says more about me than it does about them.' 'I can always do my personal best when I play.' 'I am the only one who can take responsibility for my feelings.'

- Watch what they do and how they do it. Ask yourself the question: 'What has to be true for them to be doing and saying what they are doing in the way that they are doing it?'

- Put yourself in their shoes to find out what has to be true to be acting in the way they are acting. (This skill is explained in more detail in NLP *at Work*.)

VALUES

What prompted you to read this book? What do you want to get from it? What is important to you about how it is written and how it is presented? The answers to these questions are determined by your values.

Whatever you do or say or think, what is important to you in any of those areas will lead to your values. Your values are the answer to the question: 'What is important to you?' They are the underlying needs that motivate you to do what you do in the way that you do it.

What is important to you?

A corresponding need or value drives each of the following behaviors:

- Jim was a delegate on one of my courses. He argued with just about every point that I put forward. He challenged ideas that the rest of the group presented. And if someone agreed with him he often disputed their reasons! Jim explained that he loved a challenge and his father had always valued a good argument. These values determined the way that he behaved.

- Lorraine values people. She feels that respect of people is important. She often gives advice on image and can always find out how to bring out the best in people. She is one of the best people coaches I know. She values learning and growth.

- Pat always anticipates what others' needs are. She is seen to be thoughtful and considerate. She has the ability to put herself into others' shoes in order to understand how they might be feeling and what they might need at any point in time and how they might want to be treated. On a training program she found the words to describe what was important to her – human kindness.

Ask!

To find out someone's values, ask them! Ask them: 'What is important to you about that?' This question typically changes the quality of the conversation; it is a level-changing question. The more you ask it, the more you will get to a person's core values. You may find that as you get closer and closer to these core values the other person finds it harder and harder to put words to them – they become more of a feeling.

IDENTITY

What kind of person are you? How do you think of yourself? Do you have an image and sounds and feelings attached to this identity? What labels do you give yourself if you are asked for a description? What are the unique circumstances that make you you? What is your inheritance, your birthplace and your heritage? What unique talents have you inherited and learned? How would someone describe you to differentiate you from anyone else?

I was running a program designed to enhance the participants' sensitivity. The goal was that they would become more sensitive and therefore more responsive and connected to people, both within the organization and to their clients. It was a program for which I had not established the ground rules as well as I might. In particular, I had not done enough preliminary work with the MD, who nevertheless came on the program. He struggled with the notion of becoming more sensitive and had difficulty putting himself into others' shoes. Eventually he came up to me and said: 'You know Sue, I am just not a caring person.'

The comment he gave me was at the level of identity. Working at the level of capability was a waste of time for him. His thinking would need to be shifted at a completely different level.

'I am not a caring person' is an identity statement. You can usually rely exactly on the words that people use. There will be some labels that are enabling, in that they open up choices and allow the owner of the label to grow and learn. 'I am a learner' is one of these. Equally, there are identity statements that are inhibiting, for example 'I am an unlucky person'. Of course, it is how the owner of the label reacts to its existence that will influence their behavior and their experience. Nevertheless, identity statements are overriding in the way that they influence all the levels below them in the logical levels of change model.

I have come across some people who have illness coded into their identity: 'I am an asthmatic.' This has

What kind of person are you?

quite a different effect to saying: 'I have asthma.' One is an expected permanent state and the other a transient behavior. And openness to cures and changes in state are influenced accordingly.

PURPOSE

Purpose can be an emotional word, meaning all sorts of things to different people. It is without doubt the most important aspect that many people will ever address in their lives; if indeed they do. Interestingly enough, the people that I have admired and modeled, people who excel in what they do, have often had a sense of purpose – some idea or at least a question that they have for themselves at this level of their thinking.

There is no room for self-consciousness

One of my discoveries in exploring this level for myself is that once you have a purpose that goes beyond yourself, you lose any self-consciousness that can otherwise restrict you from using your true capabilities and being fully who you truly are. Top performers have no room for self-consciousness. To give of their best they seem to have the ability to lose themselves. They do it without thinking about it.

This level is in many ways the antithesis of the level before, identity; and indeed some may say that this is about other rather than self. Purpose goes beyond self and is the place where self is no more.

So I do have questions to offer for you to explore this level, but you may find that many people do not have an answer. It may be that your question is the first time that they have asked themselves about this level in their thinking. The questions are:

- What is your purpose in life?
- What are the bigger systems to which you consider yourself to be connected?
- What value do you seek to add to those bigger systems?
- What do you want to give or in what way do you want to

be there for others?
● What is the legacy that you want to leave when you die?

I recommend that you take particular care to ensure that you have rapport with the other person before embarking on an exploration of this level.

THE WHOLE PICTURE

It is the whole picture that is of value when modeling. So often training of the past has emphasized the techniques, the levels of environment, behavior and, more recently, capabilities (sometimes referred to as competencies). It is with the beliefs, values, identity and level of purpose that you have the whole. Combinations of these levels make up the strategies for how we do what we do.

Traditional training emphasizes techniques

Some people experience this model as a journey from one level to another. When you have sorted out the material things in your life, then the question arises of what to do with them and how to make best use of them. Maybe then you progress to how to make the most of yourself and how to use what talents you have, and even how to discover where and how you show talent. Then perhaps you begin to wonder what is important in life. Certainly, my experience of those involved with personal development has been to see them climb this ladder having found the answers at one level, only to find a multiplication of those answers in new questions at the level above.

Modeling is based on a desire to learn about ways of being in the world, which may be currently unfamiliar to you. Modeling is without judgment. It is a state of curiosity. I wonder what you are thinking about that?

Once upon a time there was a Chinese emperor whose daughter was about to celebrate her seventh birthday. He decided that rather than surprise her, she was old enough to know what she wanted as her birthday present. So he asked his daughter, saying that it was his desire to give her anything she wished.

'I'd like the moon,' she replied. The emperor was shocked, but having promised her anything she wished he summoned his best engineer and told him that his task was to get the moon for his daughter. The engineer was apprehensive but enrolled a workforce to build a bamboo tower to reach the moon. The structure reached into the sky, but the taller it became the more unstable it was and eventually it collapsed, killing 50 men who were working on it at the time.

The emperor was furious and exploded at the engineer: 'Not only have you failed to get the moon for my daughter but you have killed 50 of my men in the process.' He executed the engineer.

The leading scientist in the land, who was somewhat shaken by the engineer's failure, was now summoned by the emperor with the same request. But he was a very clever man and he decided to use the latest technology to carry out the task. He built a rocket to circle the moon and with a large hook pull it back to earth. Eventually he launched the rocket with some of the best technical people he could find. But the rocket had no sooner been launched than it blew into 1000 pieces, killing the whole crew. The emperor was even angrier than before and executed the scientist.

The emperor turned in frustration to the philosopher and gave him the task of getting the moon for his daughter. The philosopher thought carefully and went to the emperor's daughter. 'I hear that you want the moon for your birthday,' he said to her.

'Yes I do,' she replied.

'What is the moon?' he asked her.

She replied by holding out her hands: 'It is a big white ball about this big.'

So he found a big white ball exactly the size that she had indicated and gave it to the emperor for him to present to his daughter. Everyone lived happily ever after.

THOUGHT PROVOKERS

1 Think of someone with whom you have some difficulty. What is it that they do that you find to be a problem? Now ask yourself: 'What is the skill that they are using [one that you genuinely admire even though you don' t like the behavior] that enables them to behave in this way?'

2 What is important to you in what you do with what you have read in this chapter? How will you go about satisfying that need?

3 Think of someone you really admire. Put yourself in their shoes and ask yourself what has to be true to be acting in the way that they do.

4 Think of the last conversation/exchange you had with someone. What would you say is the legacy that you left with them at the end of the conversation?

5 Look around you now. How is your environment an expression of who you are as a person and what is important to you?

6 Think of the results that you have in your life right now. To whom do you attribute these – to others or to yourself? If what you have are what you consider to be achievements, then do you feel that is the result of luck, God or other people? If what you experience is failure and frustration, do you look to yourself, do you blame others or some higher power?

7 Of what community do you consider yourself to be a part and what is your role in this community?

8 When you look in the mirror, who do you see?

8 Environmental Metamessages

> Within this thin wafer of bread is caught up symbolically the labor
> of plow and of sowing, of harvest and threshing, of milling, of
> packing, of transportation, of financing, of selling and packaging.
> Man's industrial life is all there.
>
> Wilford O Cross, *Prologue to Ethics*, 1963

Your environment is a mirror to your internal world

ALL environments tell a story. Whatever your environment, it is a mirror to your inner world. Your surroundings are an expression of decisions you have made, compromises that you have agreed to, goals you have achieved, desires and obligations. Look around you now. What does your environment say about you? In what way is it a metaphor for who you are? Do you like what you have, or not? What does your environment mean to you?

Everything about your environment communicates a 'metamessage' to people who experience it. It is this metamessage that creates the most meaningful impression. An example of a conflicting metamessage would be to say that you have an open door policy but in practice always to keep your office door shut. An aligned metamessage would be to be a provider of leading-edge technological solutions and to be at the forefront in the way you use these in your own environment.

A company's premises constitute a metaphor for the company itself and provide a source of data that you can use for modeling. It requires only observation to collect this valuable wealth of clues.

WHAT TO LOOK FOR

Essentially, the environment is anything outside the person. For a company this may include its buildings, the style of its offices, the surrounding area. However, it also includes the materials used – the stationery, the way letters are written and addressed.

I received a letter from one of my longstanding suppliers on which my name was misspelt and the letter arrived in a window envelope with an address label stuck over the window.

I cannot be sure what this means or why the company has done it unless I ask someone there. Nevertheless, it forms an impression. I make unconscious judgments about the company based on these details, just as I would do with someone's non-verbal behavior. Awareness of these clues will allow me to establish how they connect with other data I may discover in other phases of the modeling process. I can form some temporary theories and questions whose significance may become apparent later.

For example:

Every environment tells a story

- Is the company losing the personal contact it previously had with its customers?
- Is it watching costs or cutting corners by using up old supplies?
- Is it unconcerned about its image or is it unaware of how it may be perceived by its customers?
- Is it careless?
- Is it training its staff to maintain its standards?

- Is it under such pressure that it is losing touch with the details of the business?
- Does it care about me, its customer?
- Are people within the business communicating with each other?

Every detail reflects something of the inner workings of that company. Ultimately, the details are an expression of the person who heads up the organization. The external signs are a statement about how they communicate their values and indeed what their values are. They are an expression of the relationships they have with the people who work with and for them. The external symbols point to what internal conflicts may exist within the individual and therefore within the company.

Everything is an example. Some notable ones for me include:

- the 'welcome home' card sent by the holiday company
- the rubbish behind the desk of the airline check-in counter
- the latest equipment on each employee's desk
- the rabbit-hutch offices of development staff
- the dead flowers in the vase on the reception desk
- the clear directions sent to guide me to the company premises
- the bowl of fruit on the table in the meeting room
- the marble staircase down to the senior managers' parking bays and the scuffed rubber one that proceeded to the floors reserved for the cars of the rest of the staff
- the Japanese Koi in the pond outside reception
- the height of the reception desk

The key is observation

Each piece of data is a clue to the structure of the company and the people who run it. The key is to observe; to be sensitive to what you see and to note it and its possible implications.

UNCONSCIOUS THINKING

Most of our assumptions and meanings are formed in our unconscious thinking. This is influenced predominantly by the suggestions carried in what we see and hear rather than the content of what we notice or what is said.

For example, those companies that have posters on the wall showing their company mission statement and values may believe that this is a reminder to all who work there and all who visit. However, the metamessage that may override this is that 'we need to be reminded'. In particular, the company whose staff charter was displayed on the wall and read 'we welcome all criticism' implied that there would indeed be criticism, as opposed to feedback or learning.

When I was being shown round one company, my guide proudly showed me the floor of operators trained with the latest equipment to handle customer complaints. The company was clearly very proud of its sophisticated and extensive environment for dealing with complaints with the utmost speed. What it failed to realize was that I was horrified by the metamessage communicating the vast number of complaints it unquestionably expected and got.

What is the metamessage?

CONTRASTING METAMESSAGES

We approach the office premises of our potential new client, Intuitive Systems. It is a standard new purpose-built block behind the High Street in Stevenage Old Town. We enter the reception area and immediately notice that this company has chosen to use space differently to many of the others with similar buildings. There is an open waiting area with richly textured and deep-colored sofas. The receptionist is seated behind a highly polished wood reception desk with a high front. She greets us courteously and asks us to take a seat while she calls our contact. We sink into the soft sofas and notice that there is a PC with which we can access introductory information about the company. On the walls surrounding us are annual photos of the full team of company employees.

Using space differently

This company had been chosen as a model of excellence for others in the same field of software development. It is outperforming most of its competitors and is growing steadily. It has the style of a family company and receives tremendous loyalty from all its employees.

We were curious to know how this company had achieved the kind of success that it had. Its growth rate was unusual for the kind of market it was in. Most organizations of this nature had an erratic growth pattern or experienced a meteoric rise and subsequent depression. This company wanted to enhance its success further, hence the modeling was being carried out to establish what had constituted success to date. Although its managers were already aware of what made a difference, they recognized that there were some elements of this success that were outside of their conscious awareness. They also recognized that there were aspects of managing the business that they had not embraced simply because 'they didn't know what they didn't know'.

They didn't know what they didn't know

Our first impressions were important here and the managing director asked us for them too, which in itself was a feature of the company's culture.

Our observation of the difference in the way it had organized the reception area was reflected in its goal of running its business differently to many others in the same field. It combined family values with the world of high-tech. This was suggested in the company team photos around the walls. It cared about its staff and their respective families. It is one of the few companies that encourage delegates on courses to bring along a friend or a member of their family if they so wish.

The company paid attention to style, not only in the furnishings but also in the materials that it used to present itself. Its staff put themselves into their customers' and suppliers' shoes in order to meet their needs. The PC with the introductory information about the company was an example of this. Not only was the way this information was presented thoughtful, but care was shown in where they had placed it in the reception area.

One of the areas we identified with them as being in need of attention was their face-to-face people-handling skills. A clue to this had been the reception desk, with its barrier between the receptionist and us. This was a metaphor for the way that staff generally dealt with other people. Interpersonal skills were not their strength and this became the theme of their development training.

An interesting contrast to the previous experience was a visit to the site of a company with which we were already working. I had not been to this site before, even though I had worked with the company for a couple of years. I had difficulty finding it, as the sign showing the company name was not prominent. When I eventually did find the entrance I turned in and was stopped at the security box and asked for identification. Once cleared, the security officer directed me to some building that I could barely distinguish at the back of the site. Seeing my puzzled look, he suggested I follow the car that had entered just before me.

The road went through an expanse of wasteland, which I assumed had once supported the manufacturing plants of old. I arrived at a building at the far side of the site. There was a new façade covering an old building. I entered the reception area, which resembled a doctor's waiting room with a sliding glass screen between me and what I assume was the reception office.

The wasteland told the story

This company had devolved from its parent organization and was faced with the challenge of changing its outdated practices and finding a competitive and different way of working that would help it build new markets for the future. The wasteland told the story of the demise of engineering in the UK. The fact that it was still on view as wasteland was also significant. It reflected both a decision not to lose sight of the past and an absence of action to change the image the company presented to both the outside world and its own employees, who were reminded every day of the recession in their industry as they drove to work.

The building's façade was a metaphor for the attempts that had been made to update people's thinking and approach to the business. However, there were aspects of management style that were not only not being addressed but that were being positively avoided.

The glass screen in the reception indicated the glass wall that did indeed exist as an interface between the company and the outside world. There was little if anything that constituted 'reception' of external contacts into the company.

There was a tribe of islanders who lived on a remote island and had never been beyond the immediate waters of their home. One day a large ship that had deviated from its intended course anchored around the headland from the main beach on the island and the ship's crew ferried themselves to the shore on small boats and landing craft. The islanders greeted them enthusiastically and asked where they had come from and how they had traveled there, as they could not understand how the visitors' small boats could have weathered the rougher seas further offshore. The sailors explained that their main boat was anchored offshore and that was the boat in which they had journeyed. The islanders were very curious and the sailors took them by land to the headland where they could see the boat. But the islanders could not see it, no matter how often the crew pointed it out to them. The islanders had no concept of boats larger than their own fishing craft and they literally could not see the sailing boat. This boat was outside of their experience and continued to be so.

THOUGHT PROVOKERS

1   Look around you now. What is present in your
    surroundings? What characterizes your environment? Is
    it inherited and if so what decisions have you made to
    accept it or to change it? How is your environment a
    metaphor for the patterns you run in your life? How is
    your acceptance or influence of your surroundings
    symbolic of the decisions you make concerning the
    other bigger systems of which you are a part – for
    example your team, your organization, your family?

2   Visit your company as if you were an outsider. If possible,
    walk in the footsteps of someone who is a guest or a
    visitor. Walk where they walk. Pay attention to those
    things to which you notice them paying attention. What
    are you drawn to? What do you hear? What impressions
    of your values do these things give and how are they
    characteristic of patterns in the culture of the company?
    Notice especially how the space is used, how open or
    closed the area is, how easy it is to make contact with
    the people you want to reach, what is the decoration, and
    what accessories there are. What state are the
    surroundings in? What are people saying?

3   Invite feedback from your visitors to establish their first
    impressions of your company. Ask them what they paid
    attention to and what significance they placed on what
    they saw and heard and felt. Ask them what
    impressions they formed instantly and to what extent
    these impressions changed subsequently.

Part Two

Applying NLP to Business

The Applications of NLP to Business   9

If you ain't living it, it won't come out your horn.

Charlie Parker

*W*HEN I attended my initial NLP training more than 10
years ago, I was struck by the potential parallels
between the approaches used in the most powerful
personal therapy and the needs for organizational change.
In fact, I would go so far as to say that the needs are
identical and related. If the style of the managing director
of a business is primarily to think about problems, then it
follows that the culture of the business will be the same. To
change the business, it will be necessary to change the
style of the way it is managed.

Personal therapy parallels organizational change

The secrets of success in formulating and achieving
personal outcomes are no different to the thinking that
contributes to a great corporate vision. The approach to
resolving internal conflict and stress parallels techniques
for building bridges between members of a team or
between departments. The thinking and questions that
lead to alignment with oneself provide the recipe for
success for a congruent organization.

I would in fact go further than this and say that I believe you first of all have to apply these principles to yourself before expecting them to work in the organization as a whole. The changes that you make within yourself will ripple out to the whole organization. We are individually an expression of the bigger system of which we are a part.

CHOICE OF APPLICATIONS

I am often asked where and when to apply NLP. It may sound glib, but the answer is anywhere and at any time you choose. If what you want is to understand the structure of what works, there is no situation to which you cannot apply the thinking and the technique. When you read the case studies in the following chapters I hope you will begin to realize that the methods used in one could be applied equally to another. What matters is what works; hence the subtitle of this book:

'How to model what works in business to make it work for you'

I have chosen a cross-section of applications, but there are hundreds and thousands more. The real skill comes not in copying these but in developing the skills to provide your own unique case study. Every person I see in my one-to-one coaching sessions is unique, runs unique patterns and has unique insights. This is the beauty of modeling. It is both a celebration of our unique contributions to the world and a delight in discovering them.

Modeling is a celebration of our unique contribution

One of the most widespread applications of NLP to business has to be in the area of building relationships. The financial, task or hard side of business is becoming more and more difficult to predict in a changing global environment and is certainly beyond our control. Where we do have the potential to outreach our achievements of the past is in the way in which we relate to each other. Do you know of a relationship that does not have potential for improvement? Rather than concentrating our attention on ways of cutting back, we could be fixing our gaze on the riches yet to be harvested. In so doing, we not only obtain excellent business results but we enhance the quality of our own and others' lives at the same time.

Chapter 10, Relationships through rapport, explores how NLP is improving the quality of customer service, using the example of National Westminster Bank. The skills of building and maintaining rapport as a way of enhancing the quality of the way we handle our customers has to be top of the list of important themes for business development programs.

One revolution of the last few years has come from the concept of the learning organization, detailed with such impact by Peter Senge in his book *The Fifth Discipline*. The name and the idea may be well worn by now, but success in its implementation is not. NLP is the embodiment of learning and fits hand in glove with the ideas that Peter Senge and all the subsequent authors on the subject promote. I believe the work that Gene Early and I have developed on the learning organization within is at the leading edge of thinking on this subject. I have found it to be one of the most profound sources of personal development in my own life.

NLP and the learning organization fit hand in glove

Chapter 11, The learning organization within, starts with my own initial failure to realize that we are all a part of the systems that we condemn and it is this realization that can change the world and the way we experience it. I use the example of a family business, Altro Floors, a company that has sustained gradual and continuous growth over many years. I have also included the work that is being done by Spar Nord, a Danish bank, which is revolutionary in the kind of investment that it is making in the development of its staff.

Watch any team performance and it is those teams which act as one that find a winning streak. The team might be as small as two – rider and horse, or driver and car. If the members of a team act as one they have the means to draw on that extra that makes a world of difference. It is the same in business. Only when we have the team within working together in harmony and passion can we achieve the same with the team around us.

In Chapter 12, The inner team, I have included examples of teams who have had the willingness to challenge themselves to learn in this way – Stephen Redgrave and Matthew Pinsent, the British Olympic rowing champions, and Portland Holidays, a company from a volatile business with extremely tight margins.

One of the first applications of NLP to business was in sales. So often the forerunner in anything new, the sales team at BMW used NLP to bring consistency to their achievements as long ago as the late 1970s. Since then the expectations for anyone in sales have rocketed and what was appropriate a few years ago is no longer relevant. 'Selling is dead, long live relationships' seems to be the cry of the enlightened salesforce. So how are some of these sales teams (some who have been around for quite a few years) opening their doors to new ways of building contacts, and in some cases relationships, for life?

In Chapter 13, Personal selling skills, I examine how two big companies, ICL and Unisys, are ringing the changes through their personal selling skills programs.

Those who teach with skill are those who excel at what they do

Several years ago when I worked for ICL I remember the introduction of distance learning. I can recall a shudder of fear passing through the training department in anticipation of future redundancies. Yet here we are, more than 15 years on, and there is still no substitute for the facilitation that a skilled tutor can offer. Some of my most profound learning experiences have been with skilled tutors – people who were able to guide me and push me to go beyond the comfort zones that I was hesitating to leave. I remember hearing a long time ago the expression: 'Those who can, do. Those who can't, teach. And those who can't teach, teach teachers.' That may have been true in the past, but now the opposite is the case: those who teach with skill are those who excel at what they do. And those who teach others have the rare combination of technical skill and the ability to pass that skill on to others and allow them to find their own excellence.

PricewaterhouseCoopers attracts the best people in its field, so those whose calling it is to tutor those people are pretty special. I didn't realize how special until I embarked on a modeling project at the company. For this reason I have dedicated Chapter 14, Exceptional tutoring, to describing how they do what they do. It is no surprise either that the model at the base of this work is also one of the most powerful in highlighting what really works.

NLP was derived from observing some of the most skillful psychotherapists at work with their clients; now we are applying the same principles to the one-to-one coaching of business leaders. We are covering business issues as well as personal issues, but the approach is the same. Personal development is business development. Personal growth is business growth. Wealth of personal experience is business riches. Success comes from within, so where better to start than with yourself, especially if you happen to be the leader of the business or a team? Your personal development plan translates into the team's or the business's development plan.

Personal growth is business growth

Chapter 15, High-performance coaching, is in part a description of three people and what happened in their one-to-one sessions, and in part a transcript of the language used and the impact of challenging language patterns. Every session is unique, as every person is unique. High-performance coaching is modeling on a one-to-one basis. I have changed the names to protect the innocent!

I have recently had a change of staff in the support team who answer the calls for me and follow up enquiries. This has highlighted for me the variety in the quality of the way different people handle the phone, in particular the way they take messages. It seems such a simple task and yet there are so many subtle elements that can make the difference between a speedy, fluent and well-informed response and unchecked frustration and wasted time. More and more businesses depend for their success on the phone and the way that calls are handled. Even my local health center now has a call center (perhaps a grand-sounding word for an answering service which seems to route callers to the same receptionist whatever choice you make. I know someone who called up in good health and ended with high blood pressure as a result of the way the call was taken!)

I have included Chapter 16, Telemarketing and call centers, to reflect the growing emphasis on remote communication, especially as I am so often asked how you can pay attention to body language when you can't see the person. It was a few years ago when I realized that body language included the way we speak, as opposed to what we say. The company I have used as the example in this chapter is Save & Prosper.

Training is my life's work, so I have strong views on what makes a difference. It was the style of my early NLP trainers that made as much of a difference to me as the content of what they said. And so it should be. If we train then we have the responsibility to live out what we profess. Those who outperform the rest and win the trust and confidence of the people they train are those who expect to be held accountable for 'walking the talk'.

Chapter 17, Trainer training, highlights the difference that makes the difference between the top trainers in the world and the rest. My thinking and modeling for this have spanned 50 years – my life.

The best leaders are trainers

I do believe that all trainers are leaders and that probably the best leaders are trainers. I certainly learned from my conversations with Mike Campbell of Fujitsu Computers the source of much of the material in Chapter 18, Leadership. Interestingly enough, when I first met Mike I was his trainer.

Another company with which I have had the privilege of working for several years is Cegelec Projects Ltd. When I first started work with the people there they had just separated from GEC and were struggling to shake off the old associations and create new markets for themselves. They were far sighted enough to know that they needed to invest now in leadership for the future. They handpicked young engineers from within the business who the existing management believed had the potential to become those future leaders. In Chapter 18 I explain how we used NLP to accelerate their development and what the results have been five years later. I have also highlighted in this chapter a few of the simple but powerful techniques used by the Academy for Chief Executives to continuously support and grow the leaders who are their members. And finally, I include a company with which I am currently working, the Yellow Submarine – a model of leadership in its aligment between what it says it stands for and what it does and the manner in which it conducts its business.

TA, MBTI AND NLP

There are and have been many approaches to understanding and improving on the way we know and develop ourselves. I want to explore two of these to conclude this chapter, transactional analysis and the Myers-Briggs Type Indicator, and how they relate to NLP.

Transactional analysis (TA) was at the height of its popularity in the 1960s, offering an understanding of the different roles that we adopt in relationships – Parent, Adult and Child. TA was refreshing in the way it explained why we are the way we are and how these patterns in our history affect the way that we behave today. You may have heard of the famous book on the subject, *I'm OK, You're OK* by Tom Harris. The title in many ways reflects the goals of TA, which are for us to be OK with ourselves and for others to be OK too, even though they may be different.

At the heart of transactional analysis is the categorization of Parent/Adult/Child (PAC) as a means of defining how we are communicating with each other. These are known as the ego states. Ego states refer to the principal ways in which we demonstrate our state of being to the world. Quite simply, when a baby is born it knows how to show its feelings. No matter whether a baby feels good or bad it shows it. If the baby is fortunate, someone will anticipate and take care of its needs. If not, the baby

I'm OK, you're OK

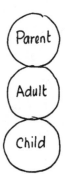

will cry, kick and do whatever it takes to get its needs met. Gradually the baby learns what works to get the response it needs. Sometimes this may be self-generated, for example it may learn that if it puts its thumb in its mouth this is a soothing way to bring comfort. Or it may learn that to kick up a fuss is a sure way of getting the attention it needs.

As the child matures it learns that there are limits. Parents say no and the child learns in all sorts of ways what the 'nos' are. It begins to learn that other people have needs too. Eventually the child learns to look for facts and to make its own analysis of the situation – it learns how to make decisions. Throughout all of this the child has also been 'recording' its experience of how its parents or the equivalent of parent figures have been responding to its needs. It has in effect made tape recordings of the 'nos' and how they were made, just as it has learned (hopefully) how to nurture its needs.

And so we have the development of the ego states:

- The child who is in total contact with its feelings and knows how to express them (Free Child).
- The child who has learned how to modify its behavior to get the approval from those with whom it must deal (Adapted Child).
- The emerging rational individual who can take an objective overview of what is going on (Adult).
- The comforting and reassuring parent who responds to the child with love and care (Nurturing Parent).
- The legislator who makes clear the rules and takes steps to make sure that others abide by them (Critical Parent).

Our preferences influence our responses

We develop these ego states to different degrees, so that rather than a balanced use of each we usually have an imbalance. We have preferences that influence how we respond to situations and how we are received by those around us. You may have a strong free child to the exclusion of something else, so that your emphasis is on getting your needs met to the detriment of the needs of others. Alternatively, you may have a strong adult, so much so that emotions rarely enter into the equation when you are making decisions. I once had a manager who when deciding on whether we could have Christmas decorations in the office considered only the budget for expenditure. And so on…

Suppose that you recognize that you have an imbalance in the development of your ego states to such an extent that it is having a negative impact on your work. NLP offers a good approach to help you learn how to reach a balance.

Myers-Briggs has almost certainly now replaced transactional analysis as a form of analysis for self-development. The Myers-Briggs Type Indicator (MBTI) – named after its developers, mother and daughter Katharine Briggs and Isabel Myers – is a means of differentiating between different personality types and the likely behaviors of each. This in itself often leads to greater understanding and acceptance of others with whom we live and work. MBTI gives us clues as to what we are based on our preferences and results, and insights into why we have the reactions that we do to situations and people. It is one of the most widely used personality type indicators in the business world today and its popularity would seem to be related to its depth and connection with the whole sphere of spirituality; as such it is widely used by the church in its work with groups, individuals and couples.

MBTI

The MBTI describes 16 different personality types and people can eventually be described, often with surprising accuracy, by one of these. In her book *Gifts Differing*, Isabel Myers writes:

When people differ, knowledge of type lessens friction and eases strain. In addition, it reveals the value of differences. No one has to be good at everything. By developing individual strengths, guarding against known weaknesses, and appreciating the strengths of the other types, life will be more amusing, more interesting, and more of a daily adventure than it could possibly be if everyone were alike.

The value of differences

MBTI looks at our preferences in four main areas. How we generate information about our world is Perceiving. How we take decisions is the process of Judgement.

First, taking the element of perception, we use our senses externally and internally to give us information about what is there. This can be what we see, hear, touch, taste and smell at the time or remembered information. It is all Sensing, and is true of someone who likes to have an idea of precise details. Others produce information by putting together patterns and possibilities to give information on what could be – a hunch or an iNtuition ('I had an intuition, I just knew this was right'). This difference can influence to what extent someone is likely to have an idea of the precise details or whether they have a more general view (this constitutes some of the difference between small- and big-chunk thinking in NLP terms).

Second, having taken in information in one of these ways, we then decide about what we have taken in according to our preference to use a Thinking route, in which we are objective and apply logic, rules and principles, or a Feeling process, when we decide from our values, beliefs and gut feelings. Those using a Feeling process are more likely to be concerned with relationships and preserving harmony.

A third element of MBTI is to do with where we draw our energy and inspiration. If you are someone who likes your own company and who needs solitude to recharge your batteries, that points towards you being an Introverted type. On the other hand, if you seek the company of other people, then your preferred type is Extrovert.

The fourth component is to do with our preference for reaching decisions and this reflects on our lifestyle. Our style varies according to whether we prefer to have an 'open' lifestyle, a willingness to be flexible and spontaneous (Perceiving), or whether we like certainty, being someone who likes to know where they stand (Judging). Perceivers will take decisions as late as possible

– they get satisfaction from gathering information. Judgers will decide as soon as they can – they get satisfaction from the decision.

No one style is right or wrong, better or worse.

You may have heard people bandy their own or others' categorizations around: He is obviously an ISTJ (Introverted, Sensing, Thinking, Judging)! She is such a clear ENFP (Extroverted, Intuitive, Feeling, Perceiving)! You may even have heard conclusions drawn about the implications of this – 'How on earth do they get on with each other!'

Understanding our own and others' preferences gives us clarity as to why we do and do not have rapport with people in our life. We are likely to find easiest company those people whose styles are similar to our own and most challenging those whose styles differ from our own natural preferences. Imagine the working dynamics of someone who loves to fly by the seat of their pants and whose decisions are based on intuition and hunches alongside someone who relies on objective evidence and who wants certainty and structure! Not an easy marriage. NLP can help here by helping us learn how to 'match' others' styles, as well as appreciating the reasons for us and others making the choices that we do.

In addition to these examples, NLP can be used to:

- learn how to value difference
- understand our own and others' strengths
- learn how to develop personality type
- deal with mid-life crises

More than anything, NLP combined with MBTI can give amazing insights into how we do what we do and how we can develop greater flexibility and skill in everything.

No one style is right or wrong

Radio and television personality Frank Muir died while I was writing this book and many of his humorous anecdotes were replayed. One of these included his account of how, before the construction of the M25 motorway, he would travel along a windy country lane to reach his home near Thorpe. Part of this journey included an especially steep hill, at the top of which was a very sharp bend. As he was driving up the hill one day, a car hurtled around the bend towards him at top speed and scraped within a thousandth of an inch of his car. He practically froze as the car tore by. The woman already had her window down and shouted at the top of her voice: 'PIG!' He was stunned and drove on round the corner – and ran into a pig.

THOUGHT PROVOKERS

1 Think of some of the areas of your work on which you
   most depend and which you would therefore most like to
   continuously improve.
2 Which companies are models of excellence for you and
   how do you go about learning from how they make a
   difference?
3 If you were to write a book like this, which people and
   companies would you include and why?

10 Relationships through Rapport

We can only grow as people by living in relationships, by in-depth communication, and by orientating ourselves towards justice and charity. Through this attitude we learn to live in 'correct proportions'.

Catharina J.M. Halkes

*T*RADE in a local pub depends on repeat business. A high proportion of the people who call in there on the way home will make a quick decision about whether they intend to return. They may first visit it because it is convenient or looks attractive from the outside, or because it sells a beer they like, but it is usually their experience as soon as they walk in that determines whether or not they will return.

A well-known chain of pubs has recognized this and has realized that its bar staff are instrumental in the customer's decision. The company decided to explore 'the difference that made the difference' between the bar staff who attracted people back and those whose rate of repeat business was not so consistently high.

The difference lay in **rapport**, particularly the immediacy with which the bar staff built rapport with the customer. The most successful bar staff were those who could quickly sense the customer's mood or state, and then not only match that state but, if necessary, turn it around. Put simply, the successful bar staff are those who could **match**, **pace** and **lead** the customer in such a way that they left feeling good – in a resourceful state.

More specifically, these bar staff and those who were subsequently trained in the same skills could **match** the customer's language and style. They would do this by using the language the customer used and mirroring the customer's behavior. If, for example, a customer's style was subdued, they would respect this and adopt a similar quieter style. If the style was one of jokiness, then they would join in with the humor; or be equally serious if that was the customer's state. Successful bar staff do this instinctively – it is probably one of the qualities that attract them to this kind of work.

I want add a 'health warning' here. You need actually to feel the feelings for this approach to be sincere. If it is only used as a technique it will not be received as authentic. Most people are skilled in detecting incongruence in others. Matching stems from a sense of rapport with the other person and is a genuine sign of respect. The most successful training comes from working with staff who have this sense of respect, but who from lack of skill mismatch the signals they pick up from others. What the training gives them is more sensitivity to the signals that others are giving and more flexibility in the way that they respond.

A 'health warning'

Jane and Charlotte are sisters. Jane, the eldest, lives at college whereas Charlotte still lives at home. They were out for dinner together with friends and were talking about their lives in general. Charlotte was upset at the restrictions that she experienced at home – deadlines for the time she was expected home, limits on friends she could have to stay, and so on. The more she talked about this and how she felt she should now be treated as an adult, the more upset she became. She could not understand why her mother would not show more leniency towards her.

Jane tried to be objective and pointed out how much more leeway was given to Charlotte than she herself had experienced when she was living at home. Jane said that as the youngest Charlotte had always had more concessions than the rest of the family. The more Jane sought to put what she saw as the facts of the situation, the more upset Charlotte got. Although Jane spoke with a calm and factual voice, she was totally mismatching Charlotte and dismissing her perception of her experience. Charlotte pointed out that Jane was of no help to her and that it was even worse when Jane was home as she sided with their mother. Jane disagreed and said that all she was doing was pointing out how she had experienced even stronger restrictions when she was living at home.

Eventually one of the group pointed out to Jane that whatever Charlotte said she disagreed with. Jane looked shocked; she had not realized that this was the case. She thought she had been understanding and objective. Someone pointed out that every time Jane replied to Charlotte, although she might start the sentence with an apparent agreement she invariably followed this with a 'but'. Jane was mismatching just about everything Charlotte was saying and doing. The effect of this observation was that Jane became aware of herself as she did this; she became consciously incompetent, to use a term from the learning levels model. Charlotte had been saying that Jane did not see her point of view and Jane began to realize that this was indeed true. By now they were both upset, but there was a much greater sense of connectedness between them. Charlotte eventually stopped crying and they began to talk with mutual understanding and empathy.

Rapport starts with acceptance

Rapport is the key to influence. Ironic though it may sometimes seem, rapport (and influence) start with acceptance of the other person's point of view, their state and their style of communication. To influence you have to be able to appreciate and understand the other person's standpoint. What Jane did here was eventually to step into her sister's shoes and then she experienced the same feelings as her sister. The effect of this rippled out to other contexts over the next few weeks. She had recently split with her boyfriend, who she thought was 'at fault' for the breakdown in their relationship, but she found herself increasingly seeing things from his point of view.

WHAT IS RAPPORT?

Rapport is the ability to join people where they are in order to build a climate of trust and respect. Rapport is influence and these work both ways: I cannot influence you without being open to influence myself. Rapport is the ability to see eye to eye, to be on the same wavelength and to connect mentally and emotionally. Having rapport does not mean that you have to agree, but that you understand where the other person or people are coming from. You appreciate and respect what the other person thinks and feels even though it may be at odds with your own thoughts and feelings – although you often find that you do share the same opinions and values.

People like people who are like themselves in some way and it is more likely that you would choose to be in the company of someone who is like you than someone who is not. The chain of taverns mentioned earlier chose to train their bar staff in building rapport on this basis – if customers are served by someone they feel instinctively comfortable with, then they will choose to come back.

People like people who are like themselves

BUILDING RELATIONSHIPS

National Westminster Bank has 'business relationship managers'. These are poles apart from the stereotypical, gray, austere bank manager who seemed to live his life behind a polished mahogany desk in the back office, protected with several layers of locked doors from the daily goings-on in the bank. The relationship manager visits you at your home or your office to find out how you are doing. Their goal is to build a relationship in order to understand not only how your business is doing but also how you are managing that business. They do this by exploring the facts of the business and by putting themselves into your shoes, so that any advice that they subsequently give comes from a position of understanding and empathy.

Rapport works best when it is a philosophy – a way of dealing with people and a way of doing business at all times – in contrast to doing rapport as a technique in a sales meeting or when there is a problem. Having rapport as a foundation for the relationship means that when there are issues to discuss, you already have a culture in place that makes it easier to talk them through. And they are much more likely to be talked through than raised as complaints, objections or problems.

THE DISCOVERY OF RAPPORT

The skill of rapport building was one of the early discoveries win NLP. When Richard Bandler and John Grinder studied some of the leading psychotherapists of the 1970s, they discovered that each instinctively built rapport with their clients through their ability to match language, particularly the use of sensory language. They also had an ability to put themselves into the shoes of their clients in such a way that they knew were the other person was coming from. In some cases the rapport was so deep that the therapist breathed at the same rate as their client. In so doing, they connected at such a deep level that they created a climate and a relationship that allowed profound change.

Rapport can exist at any or all of the following levels.

Presenting yourself

In the way you present yourself. Every company has a culture and this is often communicated in the way members of the company dress, in what they wear and the way they wear it. If your job involves you going into other companies, then the way you choose to dress will affect the success with which you build rapport. You don't have to be identical to build rapport, but you do need to signal that you respect and can therefore share the style of the people with whom you are dealing. At a deeper level, you are communicating that you can understand where they are coming from so you can put yourself in their shoes (metaphorically speaking!).

Behaviour

In the way you behave. Matching behavior is not only about building relationships, it is about behaving in a way that the other person is most likely to understand. If your style of behavior is very different to someone else's, it will be as if you come from another planet. The book *Men are from Mars, Women are from Venus* explores the different worlds of thinking and behaving that are male and female. This may be a generalization, but it is one that seems to ring true for many couples; or perhaps more especially for those who wish to be a part of a couple!

In the skills you have. At the simplest level, people enjoy the company of those with whom they share the same interests. The interest provides a common language and a common topic of conversation. Think of the people with whom you choose to spend your time. You may find that you choose to be closest to those who have similar capabilities, people who do things with a similar level of skill and style. I enjoy selling and I enjoy the company of people that I consider to be skilled in the way they do this. And I particularly enjoy reading and listening to other authors. Anyone who is drawn to modeling will be attracted to those from whom they recognize that they can learn.

The talents you have and recognize in others stem from what is important to you – your values. By spending time with those who have similar skills, you are getting close to those who share those core values.

In the values you hold. Your values represent what is important to you. They determine how you behave, what skills you draw on, what decisions you make and how you present yourself. You probably find yourself attracted to people who share the same values as you. Commonly held values are typically what holds a team together and what gives a sense of purpose to the style of your business.

If you value honesty, you will seek out the company of those who share that value. If you find that someone does not share that value in the same way as you, then you may experience some discomfort and, in the extreme, conflict. The words we use to describe values include integrity,

Talents stem from values

Common values hold teams together

trust, openness, privacy, creativity, realism… These are abstractions and we each have our own ways of living out these values and of recognizing them in others, which may not necessarily match the way that anyone else perceives the same value.

To match someone at the level of their values, you need to discover what makes a difference or not – what has to be true for their values to be met. Someone once said to me that this is probably one of the most valuable pieces of information you can possess if you want to be successful in business or in life. What has to be true for your customers to want to do business with you? What has to be true for your suppliers to give you a prompt and efficient service? What has to be true for your team to feel that they have the guidance and direction they want from you? What has to be true for you to meet your manager's requirements of you? What has to be true for you to satisfy your shareholders? What has to be true for you to feel you are being listened to? What has to be true for your partner to know that you love them?

Shared beliefs

In your beliefs. Shared beliefs hold cultures, religions, sects and communities together. Different beliefs can be the source of conflict and war. Here we have the root of relationships that bond people throughout life – or we have the cause of strife.

Your beliefs show in everything you do. You cannot conceal your beliefs; they leak out of you in every word you utter and in every movement of your body. You can attempt to conceal them, but you can be sure that what you hold to be true at the deepest level will permeate every breath you take. Beliefs are not facts; they are emotionally held opinions that will mostly have been formed early in your life. You may find yourself drawn to someone without knowing consciously why, only to discover later that deep down they hold the same beliefs as you.

I am often asked if it is possible to change beliefs and my answer is yes. There are many ways in which you can do this or in which this happens without conscious choice. And when you do this you are changing a fundamental part of who you are – your identity. It happens and you can choose for it to happen. (This is of course my belief!)

In the kind of person you are. I have said a number of times that people like people who are like themselves. I cannot overemphasize the importance of rapport and your personal responsibility in making it happen when it has not occurred naturally. But at the end of the day we are drawn to people like ourselves, in type, in style, in interests, in behavior, in appearance, in beliefs, which all adds up to the kind of people we are. Entrepreneurs rate other entrepreneurs. Sports people value other sports people. Musicians spend time with musicians. Engineers value engineers. Alcoholics pass the time with other alcoholics. Outdoor people seek other outdoor people. We are by our very nature tribal.

Who you are

In your purpose in life. This is one of those areas that you may have explored in some depth or you may never have given it any thought. Essentially, it is the answer to: 'What for?' It concerns the legacy you leave in all that you do and by being who you are. Purpose goes beyond yourself and is concerned with what you want to give others. Achieving what you want in a way that enables or supports others to achieve what they want is at the heart of win–win in any negotiation.

You attract people who share your purpose

To me, knowing your purpose in life and following that purpose is more to do with being in rapport with yourself than it is with being in rapport with others. However, I have no doubt that if you are sure about your overriding purpose, then you will attract people to you who share that purpose and who know what you stand for. They will very likely be people who wish to support you or experience your support in achieving this end.

Many of my clients are based in London and I usually travel there by train, arriving at Paddington station. My first stop is normally Costa Coffee. First thing in the morning the bar is packed out with people queuing to buy a coffee. The staff are all Italian and the whole place is alive with their chatter, laughter and shouts. Standing in the queue is an enjoyable start to the day. I have rarely seen anyone turn away when they see the length of the queue – they are more likely to be drawn to the hubbub and seem pleased to be a part of the whole atmosphere.

Last week I left the bar having decided to drink my coffee there rather than take it with me, so I was a little later than usual and I decided to get a taxi. The queue for the taxis was the longest I have ever seen. The road system around Paddington has been rerouted and it is more difficult for the taxi drivers to enter and leave the station. Fortunately, I had allowed plenty of time to get to my destination so I joined the queue. It was cold and very windy and some people were dressed for a holiday trip rather than a bone-chilling wait at the perimeter of a busy station. I had been in the queue for 40 minutes and some people had already given up and presumably decided to walk or get the tube. I estimated that there would be a further 10–15-minute wait before I would be in a taxi. At this point, one of the British Rail staff whose job it is to ensure that people queue correctly (can you imagine a role like this in countries like Israel?) walked up and down the queue telling people that he had never seen anything like this and why didn't we give up and walk and it wasn't his fault and it was an awful job anyway! I wonder if you can imagine what I said to him when at last it was my turn and he opened the door of the taxi for me?

THOUGHT PROVOKERS

1   What clubs do you belong to, if any? What attracts you to those clubs? What do you feel towards the other members and on what are those feelings based?

2   Think of someone with whom you get on really well. In what ways are you alike? In what ways are you different? How did you get to know each other?

3   Think of someone with whom you don't get on so well. How are you alike and how are you different? What would you have to change for you to get on better than you currently do?

4   Who is the first person you would typically see when you go to work? What do you do to build rapport? What more could you do to build rapport?

5   Who do you know who shares your style of dress? Who do you know who has similar mannerisms to you? Who do you know who has the same kind and level of skill as you? Who do you know who has the same values as you? Who do you know who shares your beliefs? Who would you say is most like you as a person? Who shares your sense of purpose? Whose name appears most frequently as the answer to these questions and what is the deepest level at which you have rapport with this person?

6   Given freedom of choice, where would you spend your time tomorrow and with whom would you spend it? Why? What does this tell you about what is important to you and how you go about creating that rapport with yourself?

11 The Learning Organization Within

*The dominant fact of the twentieth century is that the entire
population of the earth is now included within a single community.
There are no more ocean barriers, no mountain barriers of any kind.
There is only one race now – it is the human race.*

Obert C Tanner, *One Man's Search*, 1989

I entered the darkened room that was the boardroom.
Spotlights highlighted the individual seating positions.
The mahogany table gleamed in the pockets of light; no
random scribblings on this table. I recognized some of the
faces grouped on the far side of the table. There were a
few nods of acknowledgment but no smiles. This was
serious stuff, obviously. I was quietly ushered to an
illuminated seat and waited my turn. Thoughts of
Christians being thrown to the lions came to mind, but I
turned to more constructive mental preparation.

I was here to brief the board on the Managing Change
courses that we had started in a few divisions of the
company. My contact had warned me that not all the board
members were in favor of these courses and she was right.
It was evident that the agenda for some at the meeting was

to tell us why we shouldn't be running such events. I presented my thoughts, to a few timid nods of approval. My time was up. My contact and I were shown out of the meeting almost as quietly as we had been shown in. 'Well, what did you think?' she asked, with a wry smile on her face.

'Dinosaurs!' I replied. 'They will be extinct in a few years' time if they continue in the same way.' I based my exclamation on my experiences of them as inflexible, dogmatic and judgmental.

'You are the dinosaur!' retorted one of my colleagues when I recounted the incident a few days later. I was shocked and then realization dawned. I was confronted with a mirror to my own patterns. 'It takes one to know one,' my grandmother used to say; she was right. We can only recognize in others the qualities, good or bad, that we have within ourselves in some way.

It takes one to know one

WHAT IS A LEARNING ORGANIZATION?

What does this have to do with the concept of the learning organization? And what role has NLP to play in all of this? In *The Fifth Discipline* Peter Senge describes the learning organization as:

'an organization that is continually expanding its capacity to create its future.'

Much of the literature on this subject will tell you what is needed to create such a culture, and there is little doubt that doing so is crucial for any business to survive and succeed, today and in the future. In fact, the organizations which are achieving this kind of culture are the ones which seem to be excelling in their particular markets. Far less of the literature can tell you how to achieve the culture of a learning organization. One exception to this is *The Fifth Discipline Fieldbook*, which details much of the work in this direction that has so far been done by organizations.

It is in the 'how' that NLP comes into its own. It offers

the structure of the thinking and the behavior that is the difference that makes the difference. Because of the emphasis in NLP on our internal world, which bears many similarities to the discipline of mental models in *The Fifth Discipline*, we are offered the means of achieving a learning organization within. It is only when we have the structure of this way of influencing our internal world that we have the means to create the same culture on the outside.

CONTINUOUS LEARNING

'The ability to learn faster than your competitors may be the only sustainable competitive advantage.'

Arie de Geus, quoted in *The Fifth Discipline*

Just as more companies commit to training programs and development plans that ensure that employees have a guaranteed amount of training and development each year, we are realizing that this is merely a drop in the ocean. The most successful learning organizations are those in which people learn continuously from everything they do. To restrict their learning to courses and books would be to use only a fraction of the available opportunities. It is our ability to learn from everything that we do, good or bad, that marks us out from the rest in our growth, our quality and our satisfaction – and ultimately in the business results that we achieve.

There is no failure, only feedback

In NLP *at Work* I referred to the belief that there is no failure, only feedback. This triggers all sorts of responses, including the cynical: 'We've had an awful lot of feedback this year, Sue!' I can appreciate this – it is a challenging belief to take on board, but one that underpins the culture of the learning organization.

An organization in which this belief prevails is one in which employees welcome and invite feedback, from whatever source. It is also a given that the receiver will explore what they can learn from what they hear. And such companies don't rely just on the feedback they receive, they actively solicit feedback as a means of knowing how they are doing, whether that be in customer service, management skills, organizational change, inter-departmental cooperation or whatever.

The members of a learning organization learn from everyday events, not just from conversations labeled as feedback, and they manage themselves to increase flexibility in their thinking and their actions. They do this on the basis that they are the only thing in a system that they can absolutely change.

THE MIRROR TO YOURSELF

What we perceive in others is a mirror to ourselves. I believe that this is one of the single most powerful sources of personal learning available today. It is this belief that is at the heart of concepts such as ownership, accountability, personal development, personal mastery, systems thinking, team learning and more. Just how does this work? As with most NLP concepts, the magic is in the meaning that we choose to put on the situations we experience. It is the meaning, if not the events, over which we have control.

I am rarely annoyed by delegates on my courses; in fact I pride myself on my ability to take learning from some of the most unusual situations and sometimes ones that other consultants might find irritating. However, there are exceptions and one notable one stands out in my thinking. I was running a course at our conference center, a beautiful converted barn and outbuildings. Next to the room in which we were doing the training is a swimming pool. It was a very warm day and some of the delegates had been for a swim in the lunch period. All had got dried and changed, with the exception of one who sat right in front of me enveloped in a wet towel and with her bare feet up on a chair to one side. I thought this was rude and inconsiderate, but I let it pass.

Later that day the same delegate interrupted a session I had just started by rummaging through her notes while I was speaking. I could feel myself getting tense, but again I said nothing. The next day she continued to act in a way that caused disruption to the sessions and was seemingly unaware of the effect that she caused. However, I noticed that no one else seemed too bothered about this. I also noticed that at the start of each session I would tense up in anticipation of what she might do next.

The last straw for me was when, just after we had started the afternoon session, she got up and walked across to the far side of the room where coffee and tea were set out and, after rattling the cups, poured herself some tea and sat down again. By this time I had completely lost the flow of what I was saying. At the end of the session, I approached one of my colleagues and expressed my frustration. Not a good example of state management! It seemed that my colleague was not bothered in the same way and asked me what it was about this delegate's behavior that bothered me so much. I explained that it was her single-mindedness and her complete insensitivity to other people that I found so rude. I was already beginning to make a connection through this question. It was my colleague's next question that did it for me. (And these questions were ones that we had been doing a lot of work on within the previous few months.) She asked me how what I recognized in this delegate was me. My initial reaction was one of horror and denial. Surely not – she was nothing like me and I was nothing like her. Nevertheless, the question stayed with me and eventually the penny dropped. I was exactly like her!

It was not her behavior that was me but the meaning I put on her behavior – the single-mindedness and insensitivity. I know I have those traits within myself; I have worked on them over time and, although I demonstrate them far less than I used to, they are still there.

I have referred elsewhere in this book to a concept that Stephen Covey presents in his book *The Seven Habits of Highly Effective People*. He explains that between every stimulus and response there is a gap, and that it is what we do in this gap that is significant in terms of influencing our state and therefore our reaction. The gap may only be microseconds, but in that fraction of time we may imagine how the situation will work out, we may have an internal conversation with ourselves, we may recall images of the past or a conversation we have had before. These internal actions are what affects the way we make meaning of our lives. It is so often the unconscious programs we run that contain the keys to the 'difference that makes the difference' in NLP. By learning to access these often previously unnoticed steps in our own and others' thinking, we will have the means to coach ourselves and others to outstanding personal performance in whatever we choose to do.

As a result, what we recognize or project on to others is what is true about ourselves. In the case of the delegate on my course, it was not that I would sit wrapped in a wet towel in the middle of someone's course, nor would I interrupt a session to get a cup of tea or coffee. What I do recognize in myself, however, is single-mindedness and insensitivity. Not at all times, I hasten to add. But when I set a goal that is important to me, I have been known to go for it without regard to other people's reactions to what I am doing. I like to think that I am aware of this now and I have some other choices about the way I go about achieving my goals. Nevertheless, I have this capacity and what we recognize in others is a reflection of the structures we have within ourselves.

Of course, what this means is that when we give feedback to someone else, we may be saying more about ourselves than we are saying about that person. We recognize the traits in others that we have the representation of within ourselves. If we did not have them, we would not be able to recognize them.

BREAK FOR LUNCH

When Len drove back to the office at midday after an intensive morning with one of his clients, he slowed as he reached the traffic lights at the end of the road. There on the park bench across from the lights was his secretary, eating her lunch. He was stunned and asked himself how she could take the time to sit there when he was up to his eyes in challenges and outstanding deadlines. He realized just how frustrated with her he had become over the last few months. She did not take on any more work than she needed to. She arrived at work promptly at 9 a.m. and left on the dot of 5. Basically, she did what she had to do and no more. Len found himself getting increasingly annoyed and wound up with her behavior, although reluctantly he also recognized that she had a busy social life with her husband. He decided to discuss the difficulties he was having with his secretary during a personal development coaching session to see if he could find any new ways in which he could influence her to take on more work.

At the start of Len's personal development program, he had identified that he wanted to have more control over his time. He worked all hours, weekdays, weekends and holidays. He switched his mobile phone off through dinner at home, but not much more often than that. Even on the drive to Italy for his 30th wedding anniversary, he had commented that the roads were good basically because the mobile phone signal was stronger than in the UK, so he could stay in contact all the way.

In raising the issue as part of his own development, Len expected to get some advice on new influencing techniques he could use to get the few members of staff who didn't work at the same hectic pace to do so. He didn't get this advice. What he did get was a realization that, far from him influencing his secretary, she had a lot to offer him. What she had was a superb ability to manage her time. It was therefore not surprising that each time he saw her using time in the way she wanted to he became totally frustrated. What he was seeing was what he would dearly love for himself; maybe not in literally the same way but in essence. So often what triggers negative feelings in us with regard to others is recognition of something that we are frustrated or angry with in ourselves.

This realization alone shifted all Len's thinking towards Melanie. He became aware that, far from being frustrated with her, he was in admiration of her. Len's subsequent appraisal with Melanie changed from what might have been a disciplinary interview to a personal development session for them both. After all, when one person in the dynamic changes so do the rest!

ALTRO FLOORS

Altro Floors is a safety-flooring manufacturer. It is a family firm that was established in 1909 and has grown successfully ever since. It now has 500 employees worldwide, with bases in the UK, Scandanavia, Germany and France. It has long been a model of excellence for other UK companies and is admired particularly for the way it has developed its employees to manage the enormous changes that have taken place, especially in the last 10 years.

In fact, 10 years ago that the company first introduced a documented performance appraisal scheme. Two of its goals were to collect information about company-wide training needs and to improve managers' abilities to develop and grow their staff. The system was designed carefully so that it would be in line with the culture of the company, rather than attempting to bolt on a system that might be more suitable for a larger and possibly more bureaucratic organization. For this reason, the forms that accompanied the introduction of the system were kept as simple and flexible as possible. There were no box markings, there was no numerical grading of staff performance.

Since the introduction of this scheme the company has grown and it has become more of a challenge for the senior management team to keep in touch with everything that is happening on the shopfloor. All staff's workloads have grown and members of the senior management team have become more distanced in their dealings with each other as a result of the pressures of the expanding business. Senior managers began to realize that although they were still conducting performance appraisals, in the main they were treating them as a 'bolt-on' to the 'real' business. They decided to address this issue by exploring

MOVING TO THE CULTURE OF A LEARNING ORGANIZATION

the way that they thought about and conducted performance management among themselves. The team decided to explore how they could make the biggest difference in moving the company to the true culture of a learning organization.

Members of the senior team (in this case the board of directors) create the culture of the business in the way they interact and behave moment to moment, not only with each other but especially with their staff. Each aspect of their behavior acts as an example to others. It is not that they don't influence, but that they are *always* influencing. What matters is whether they are being an example of the way they want others to be in the business.

Being an example of what is wanted

The team recognized very quickly that they did not fully live out the presupposition 'there is no failure, only feedback'. This is at the heart of a learning culture. To hold this presupposition means to treat every situation, every moment, as an opportunity to learn and to gain some new choices and flexibility.

The team built up a list of factors that would help them to recognize whether they were living out this presupposition to the full. They used their own experience to identify when they were blocking learning and when they were missing opportunities to learn, and this assisted them in being an example of learning for others in the company.

This list identified that they were learning when they:

- asked for feedback on anything they had done or said
- sought clarification from the feedback that the other person was giving them, as opposed to explaining why they had done or said what they had
- used the feedback they got as a means of developing their flexibility rather than seeking to shut it out in some way
- accepted that however they were perceived by another person was valid, even if it was different to the way they believed they had come across

- were curious whenever anyone offered them feedback and wanted to explore how the other person felt
- apologized for any occasion when they had upset or confused or contributed to any unresourceful state in another member of the team
- were honest in their feedback to others in the team
- checked that they had good rapport with the other person before they gave feedback
- ensured that they were giving the feedback with a desire to enhance the other person's learning as well as their own and therefore contribute to the learning and growth of the team and the business
- recognized that the feedback they gave was as much about them as it was about the other person (it takes one to know one)
- were committed to supporting the person to whom they had given feedback in such a way that they could both learn and grow and change
- accepted that they would feel uncomfortable in the process of putting feedback into practice
- agreed to support each other in implementing their respective action plans, to keep on each other's case
- recognized whenever they were tempted to say 'yes, but' or anything similar and replaced it with an open curiosity

They believed that if and when they demonstrated each of these characteristics, they would fully own the presupposition 'there is no failure, only feedback' and as such they would be continuously improving both personally and as a business.

Of course, the team also took other factors on board, including the skills of coaching and mentoring, but it was this presupposition regarding feedback that was at the heart of the learning culture.

SPAR NORD

Spar Nord is a Danish bank with a different way of thinking and a goal of increasingly becoming a learning organization. The bank's involvement with NLP consultants Straandgaard Gruppen and The Sue Knight Partnership has resulted in its now having its own NLP facilitators to train 1100 employees in taking ownership of their own personal development. So far nobody has lost contact with reality, and training leader Winnie Flensborg has been a central figure in the banking world's focus on effectiveness and the staff members who must deliver the goods.

Spar Nord was the first company in Denmark to create an internal NLP training program for specially chosen staff members. The composition of the team was based on the idea of being able to train branch managers as NLP facilitators and in this way let them take ownership of the decentralized organizational development.

At the time of writing Spar Nord has 20 NLP facilitators, also called personnel trainers. They have all passed an 18-day basic education in NLP, for which they have received a certificate. Their aim is to create a culture centered on the learning organization as they continually exchange experiences and insights.

From TQM to NLP

Spar Nord has a tradition of investing in training aimed at the 'softer' values. Its aim is to create a balanced organization and it is for this purpose that it uses NLP. Winnie Flensborg says:

'One becomes lopsided from focusing only on, for example, credit and management systems. We work with ethical accounting and we have always taken into consideration the human factor. Production challenges can be managed with total quality management and business process reengineering and to deal with the mental challenges that accompany these we use NLP.'

The challenges of creating synergy between TQM, BPR and NLP occur at all levels in the company. However, you do not necessarily become a learning organization in a day and Winnie Flensborg believes that it will be a zigzag path to reach that goal. It may be zigzag, but she believes it will be worth it.

Once upon a time there was a man who had led a good life and when he died he went to heaven. On arrival at the gates of heaven, he was met by a guardian who introduced himself and welcomed him to the next world. However, before leading the man through the gates of heaven, the guardian said: 'I know this might seem strange, but you have a choice. Whether on earth or here beyond life, people can choose where they want to be. Some choose to live in hell and some choose to be in heaven.'

The man looked puzzled and asked: 'Why would anyone choose to be in hell? I can't imagine that would appeal to anyone.'

The guardian replied: 'You'd be surprised. You don't have to decide right now – you can take a look at both if you like and then you can make up your mind.'

The man agreed and the guardian led him through a door and down a long corridor. As soon as they had gone through the door the man could smell the most tantalizing aromas, rich spices and mellow flavorings. His mouth was watering. Eventually they came to a window and inside were beautiful tables laden with the most magnificent food you could imagine. He turned to the guardian and said: 'So this must be heaven – I have never before seen or smelt such a wonderful banquet. It is beyond anything I have ever experienced.'

'Well, no,' said the guardian. 'In fact this is hell.' At that moment the man noticed the people around the room. They were emaciated, with grey complexions and drawn, hard expressions on their faces. He could not immediately see what was wrong. And then he watched someone trying to eat. This person's arms were rigid and whenever they managed to get hold of some of the food and tried to put it in their mouth, they could not bend their arms and the food fell on the ground.

'How dreadful,' the man exclaimed, 'to have this banquet before you and not to be able to partake of it! Let me see heaven.'

The guardian led him away and further down the corridor there wafted more delightful aromas, but no more enticing than the ones before. And when they looked through this next window there again was a magnificent banquet of food. When the man looked at the people there he was shocked to see that they also had rigid arms. But these people were healthy. They looked happy and content and they most certainly didn't look undernourished. Some of the people approached the table and proceeded to pick up some of the food. He wondered what would happen when it dropped on the floor as they tried to bend their stiff arms and then he saw what happened. Instead of trying to put the food into their own mouths, they turned and placed it in someone else's mouth. It didn't matter that they couldn't bend their arms — they fed each other.

THOUGHT PROVOKERS

1 Think of someone with whom you don't get on as well as you would like. What is it about them that you don't like or that triggers a negative response in you? How are you the same as them? (Maybe not in literally the same behavior, but in the meaning that you put to the behavior.)

2 When did someone last give you feedback? How did you react to it? With what result? What have you done differently since that is a measure of your growth?

3 To what extent do you feel that people around you can give you feedback? To what extent do you invite it? How do you do this? To what extent do you discourage it, either by what you say or by how you respond?

4 If someone holds a different perception to your own of what you have done, to what extent do you believe that their opinion is valid and worthy of exploration?

5 How do you feel when you don't achieve a target you have set yourself and what do you do when that happens?

6 How do you feel when you do achieve a target that you have set yourself and how do you seek to learn in such a way that you achieve a better result if possible next time?

7 When did you last unconditionally praise someone?

8 When did someone last unconditionally praise you?

9 To whom are you committed to support in their development and growth – at work and in your family? How do you demonstrate this commitment?

10 With whom do you have the sort of rapport that enables you to give feedback in such a way that you know it will be accepted?

11 With whom do you not have this sort of rapport and what can you do to get it? Who do you think has the responsibility to build this rapport?

The Inner Team 12

They all knelt together and suddenly — not a barrier of any kind remained, not a sundering distinction in the whole throng; but every life flamed into the other, and all flamed in to the one Life and were hushed in ineffable peace.

Zephrine Humphrey, *The Edge of the Woods and Other Papers,* 1913

IN 1997 one of my associates, Mike, died aged 53. His death was not a surprise, as he had become increasingly ill over the previous year, but it was a shock. We had hoped and prayed for him to recover to the very last moment and had even thought that he was beginning to improve. It was only when I went to his funeral that I really appreciated what he had brought to us as a team and to life in general. Most of my reactions to him, as they are to many other people, were at the level of the jobs we were engaged in at the time. I often responded in the context of the rush of our growing business and I felt frustrated that he didn't always want to join me in this rush.

PRESUPPOSE THAT WE ARE ONE

I have since come to the conclusion that one of the most important roles that we can fulfill as a member of a team is to respond to people for who they truly are. I knew this before in my head, but not always in my heart. What is important is to see what they really bring – to go behind the behavior and to respect and accept them for the truth of who they are.

There are many NLP presuppositions that connect with this and they can be read as glib statements – or we can look into the depths of their meaning and what they can bring to us in the way we go about our lives. The presuppositions that you will find in any textbook on NLP were discovered as a result of modeling people who had

An outstanding ability to connect with others

an outstanding ability to connect with others as a part of their work and in life. They formed the backcloth to the profound influence that these people had and still have on those with whom they come into contact.

It was on the first evening of my first course in NLP that I heard this set of presuppositions. They made sense, but I couldn't really see what all the fuss was about and why we dedicated a whole evening to them. I have changed my opinion since, as I have with many of the other NLP ways of thinking that I was presented with then. Far from feeling that an evening is too long too explore the meaning and significance of these presuppositions, I feel now that a lifetime is probably too short.

I have set out a longer set of presuppositions in my book NLP *at* Work, but the ones I find particularly pertinent to the context of teamwork are the following.

THE MAP IS NOT
THE TERRITORY

What this means to me is that we are each unique – in the way we think and in the way we behave, particularly in the way we perceive situations and life. No one is more right than anyone else. Everyone's perception is valid and is the truth for them. It is arrogant to believe that your perception is any more right than that of anyone else. To hold this presupposition (and some hold it as a belief) is to respect everyone for who they are and to seek to understand what it is like to be them. When we take this stance, we make a connection with them and we have choices about what we do with that connection. By holding this presupposition, we are open to influence as well as being in a position to influence. Whatever we do we do from a position of rapport. We do not have to agree with someone to be in this place, but this does enable us to understand where they are coming from.

We make the best choice available to us at the time we make the choice. It may not be a good choice or an admirable choice – indeed, there are times when it may be a positively damaging choice – but it is the best one based on our state, our feelings, our skills, our resources, our needs, our beliefs, our limitations, our upbringing, our influences, our environment, our sense of self-worth, our feelings about our identity and our known or unknown purpose in life. Our unconscious, sometimes with the help of our conscious mind, puts the whole lot into the pot and acts. It comes up with the best it can to satisfy all of the above in the decision it makes. When we accept this presupposition, we understand that and we open the possibility of really understanding what is under the surface. We can begin to truly connect with others whoever they are and whatever they may have done.

PEOPLE MAKE THE BEST CHOICES AVAILABLE TO THEM

I used to work with someone years ago when I was in IT technical training who found most of the groups of course participants that he trained 'as thick as two short planks', to use his expression. In all the time I knew him and through all the occasions he experienced this, he never once noticed the common denominator – himself! To hold the presupposition that the meaning of the communication is the effect is to believe that the quality of your communication is measured by the results it achieves. If you are understood in what you say, then that is the measure of the communication. If people are confused or disagree with what you say, then that is also the meaning of your communication.

THE MEANING OF THE COMMUNICATION IS THE EFFECT

And it doesn't stop at communication. For communication substitute leadership, team membership, friendship, parenting, loving, partnering, existence! What you experience around you in the effects that you have is the meaning of how you are being. If people are hostile to you, it is feedback on how you are being with them. If people are ignoring you, it is feedback on how you are being not only in that moment but as a result of how you have been with them over time. If people like you and seek out your company, it is feedback on how you are relating and have related to them. If people ask your advice, it is feedback on how you influence and have influenced them.

Whether you hold these views as temporary thoughts (presuppositions) or as permanent beliefs, the effect of doing so will be that you will own your experience and not blame others. It is likely that you will feel relaxed with others whoever they are and however they behave. It does not mean that you accept their behavior, but you will be in a sufficiently resourceful state to respond in a way that is most likely to benefit you both and from which you can both learn.

You can be in a resourceful state

These may be just words on a page to you, but I and all other practitioners of NLP emphasize that it is only in the living of the words that we bring them to life. As you peel away one layer of questions, you will reveal even more at another and much deeper level. And so the learning continues.

A bereavement counselor told me what she had learned about the things that really make a positive difference for people who have lost someone close to them. One young mother who had lost her first child – a boy, whom they had named Jacob – had just given birth to a baby daughter. The mother was being pushed out of the lift on a stretcher with the baby in her arms when she saw the nursing sister who had been present at her previous birth. The sister bent down and took the baby's tiny hand in hers. 'So you're Jacob's baby sister,' she said.

THE LARGER TEAM OF WHICH WE ARE A PART

At Mike's funeral I met many old colleagues that I had not seen for a long time, in some cases several years. I realized that we came together as a different kind of team on that day – one that had a different purpose to any we had had before and yet we immediately functioned as a caring, supportive, loving team without preparation and without thought. The team withstood the test of time and pain.

This is what team excellence is really about for me. It is being a member of a group of people who exist to support each other and to meet each team member's needs whatever they are and however unexpectedly they arise. And in doing this they fulfill a higher purpose and achieve their goal.

Systems thinking is becoming the fashion for how we move our businesses forward into the twenty-first century. We are looking to collaborations and partnerships to replace the competition of the past. We are exploring how we can win together, as opposed to how we can defeat and cut the legs out from under our opponents.

SYSTEMS THINKING

Systems thinking involves recognizing that we are an integral part of the whole; the meaning of the communication is indeed the effect. There are teams to which we consciously know we belong; but what of those of which we are currently unaware? Which are the bigger teams – the bigger systems of which we are an integral part and on which we are unknowingly having an influence every day of our lives? Which are the teams that we could choose to influence in a more positive and constructive way than we already do? How far out does your system extend?

The meaning of the communication is the effect

An article in a national newspaper reported on the experiences of guests on one of the Apollo space missions. They represented several different countries around the world. As the space shuttle pulled away and they got their first glimpse of Earth from space, they excitedly pointed to their respective countries as they made their orbits. After a few days when there was an even greater distance between them and the Earth, they pointed to their respective continents. And by the end of the first week when the Earth was a small globe far away in the distance, they all pointed to the Earth as one. It was this sense of interconnectedness that each person without exception reported as being the overriding insight they took from the experience.

Contrast that with the following example:

Each member of the team had their own regular place around the meeting table. The managing director always sat at the head of the table with the human resources manager (one of his colleagues in his previous company) to his right. The newly appointed sales manager sat to one side of the table away from the rest. The overseas member of the team, someone who represented a very different culture to the one they were seeking to develop for the future, sat immediately opposite the managing director at the far end of the table. The finance manager and the marketing manager sat on the other side of the table, side by side but not too close to each other.

This was a team whose meetings usually resulted in at least one of the members walking out in anger before the end. They needed a strategy for how to go forward, yet they did not have the means to stay together long enough to produce it.

I met with each of the team members one to one. Most blamed at least one of the others for the problems they were experiencing. No one considered themselves to be responsible. I encountered the infamous 'they' problem: 'They' would not listen. 'They' had to do things their own way and would not accommodate anyone else's style. 'They' were making wrong decisions and weren't running their bit of the business effectively.

The infamous 'they'

MANAGING THE INNER TEAM

When Stephen Redgrave and Matthew Pinsent won the gold medal in the Olympics coxless pairs, it wasn't the first time they had rowed the race. Without question, they had completed this race many times before in their heads. Not only had they physically practiced together, they had mentally rehearsed how they would excel as a team. Any doubt how they might support each other or work in total harmony would have cost them the race. The most successful athletes are those who recognize that they need not only physical preparation but also mental rehearsals. The race needs to be won on the inside before it can ever be won on the outside. Any moment of doubt will reflect itself in performance.

The performance of a business team depends in the same way on the thinking that goes on in the minds of the team members. The external team is an expression of the internal team.

Consider the teams of which you are a member – your project team, your management team, your company, your family and your community. As you think about each of these, what do you see, hear and feel? Are these internal teams as you would really like them to be, or are they in conflict in any way? Do you experience satisfaction and motivation as you think about them or do you feel frustration and conflict? It is this internal representation that will determine your actual experience with the team when you meet.

You are the team, you are the family. Your influence comes from within yourself. Only by influencing yourself can you influence the others around you. You cannot hope to change others without first changing yourself. And the only aspect of you that you can change and that will make a difference is your perception of what has been, what is and what will be.

You are the team

So the first step in managing the external team is to imagine the way that you would truly like the team to be working and relating to each other. Imagine the team the way you want to see it and the way you want it to be seen by others. Imagine the way you want the members of the team to be talking to each other. How would you like the team to be talking to other people with whom they interface and what would you like those people to be saying about the team? How do you want to feel and what emotions would you like the team to trigger in each other and anyone else with whom they deal? What you think is what you get, which is why the ability to imagine the results and the situations you want in exactly the way you want them is key to success.

COMMITTING TO EACH OTHER

Meeting individual needs and achieving business results

A team that excels is one in which members commit to meeting each other's needs. Often the thought that gets in the way of this is the belief that it is not possible to meet everyone's needs *and* achieve the results of the business. Nothing could be farther from the truth. Modeling top teams has shown us that teams whose members have this commitment to each other are those who not only delight in their members' company, but who also outperform any similar teams in their ability to achieve business results.

Committing to meet each other's needs implies that you first find out what those needs are. They may be implied or hinted at, but not always overtly expressed. The most successful teams can be explicit about their needs as well as having the flexibility to adapt to meet them.

Straight requests do not always imply needs. If someone asks you to let them know what the results are of a task they have asked you to do, it may be because they need feedback in order to feel satisfied that the result has been achieved. You may have a member of your team whose needs are for ownership of the areas they manage and they will be precise in what they mean by ownership. You may have other members who want to know they are valued by the way they are rewarded for the work they do. This may not mean a monetary reward; don't assume that what functions as a reward for one person will function as a reward for another. It is your skill in establishing these unique criteria that will determine satisfaction for each individual member of your team.

UNCOVERING NEEDS

Ideally your team members will have thought through their needs and will be able to vocalize them – but this is the least likely situation. If they have done this, then it is just a matter of listening to them and exploring how you can each commit to supporting and meeting them.

The less desirable situation is to discover needs only when they aren't being met. For example, have you ever been in a situation when a colleague has gone into a huff or a sulk and you don't know why? You can be sure that their needs have not been met, but this is their unhealthy way of showing this. Other unhealthy ways include temper outbursts, shows of irritation, moodiness, cynicism and the like. Hopefully you won't encounter all of these, although they are not unusual in many family teams and in the worst of business teams. These sorts of ways of expressing feelings dissipate energy and motivation, which could usefully be directed towards the results that are really wanted by the organization.

Nevertheless, these are cues to be followed through. Any indication that these are happening should prompt questions along the lines of: 'What is your response?' or 'What do you need right now?' Or, depending on what result or response you want: 'What do you need in order for you to be able to… (whatever response you want)? For example, '…give me your support?' Or '…commit to this project?'

The ideal for any new team is to start with the process of eliciting needs for each other. It is very likely that everyone will not know what all of these are. It is a process that will probably have to be revisited many times, as needs do change.

The questions that you can use to determine the needs of each member of the team include: 'What is important to you about that?' 'That' may be any request the person has made, any opinion they have expressed, any decision they have made. Virtually anything is fair game for this question. You can expect to receive answers that include words like 'recognition', 'inclusion', 'a sense of achievement', 'a feeling of being valued', 'freedom to make my own decisions', 'respect'.

When interviewing the workforce of one large organization who were threatening strike action for the way

What is important to you about that?

the performance appraisal scheme had been introduced, and whose management thought the dissatisfaction was pay related, we found that the most important issue was the respect and courtesy the staff were shown. And the way in which most people wanted to be shown respect and courtesy was by being greeted when they were passed in the corridor or by being thanked when they had completed a job successfully.

By continuing to ask 'What is important to you about that?' you will find that the recipient will eventually and often quite quickly reveal some of their core values. These represent those needs that have to be met, whatever the context, in order for that person to feel satisfied.

Most needs are expressed as abstractions. Everyone puts their own unique meaning to these words. What one person means by 'fun', for example, can be quite different from what another means by the same word. To determine the unique meaning you need ask the question: 'What would have to be true for you to know/feel you were... (having fun/being valued/experiencing freedom etc.)? When you get measurable specifics, you know you are on the right track, for example if someone says: 'I know I am having fun if I am laughing at work at least once a day and I have time to have lunch with at least one other member of my team at least once a week.'

BRIDGING THE GAP

When the managing director in the earlier case study sought to have a discussion with his overseas colleague, the conversation invariably resulted in discord. They came from different cultures and had very different styles of communication, not only with each other but also with the other members of the team.

Conversations would often go along these lines:

'Bill, I'd like to talk to you about the direction we want to take as a business.'

'That's fine – I have a lot of experience of doing this. In fact, the direction we worked towards where I was based before was…'

'Yes, yes, I know you have experience of this in your previous organization, but I would like to take a very different approach to it here.'

'I understand that and I want to support you. I feel that by exploring what worked in the past as well as what didn't, we can draw some lessons that can ensure we don't make any mistakes in the way we do it this time.'

'I'd prefer to get a vision sorted out without contaminating it with anything either of us has done before. Let's clarify where we see the business going in the next two years and then we can review what we have achieved towards past goals.'

'I really don't like your suggestion that we would be contaminating our thinking. I find that insulting!'

And before long the conversation would reach an abrupt end, leaving them further behind than when they started.

So what is happening here? Each is demonstrating elements of their own style. The MD is oriented towards the future and likes to visualize. He tends to want to see the direction of the business in global terms. The other manager tends to the past and the detail. He explores his ideas through his feelings and uses language that demonstrates this. Their style of communicating is at odds with each other. No wonder they get frustrated or don't see eye to eye, as the MD would be more likely to say!

The frustrations that occur because of different styles are a common theme in teams today. However, as soon as team members become aware of what constitutes their individual styles, more often than not this is accompanied by a resulting tolerance and understanding of each other. Chapter 6 explains some of these different styles in more detail. You can adapt your style of communicating, in particular what you say and how you say it, so that it fits the style of the person you are talking to. By doing this, you are increasing the chance that they will understand and accept what you say.

Become aware of what constitutes different styles

Some of the aspects that make up different styles are the extent to which someone is:

- paying attention to problems or future goals
- either connected to and expressing their feelings or being detached and objective
- oriented towards what they see, hear or feel
- paying attention to what is not working or what is not present, as opposed to concentrating on what is working or what is present
- searching for the opposite or what is different in what is presented to them, as opposed to what is the same or similar
- procedural and oriented towards systems and procedures or based on an array of choices and options
- global and abstract in their thinking and communicating or specific and detailed
- paying attention to the past, the present or the future
- oriented towards themselves and how things affect them personally or oriented towards others and the implications for them

The most influential team members are those people who can tailor what they say and how they say it to suit the individual or the group of people to whom they are talking.

The person with the most flexibility in their thinking and behavior is the person most likely to achieve their goal.

BUILDING TEAM RELATIONSHIPS

Rapport is the necessary precursor to successful business

'Building relationships is all very well, but we can't sacrifice the time it takes to do the business.' A businessman made this comment to me only recently. It still surprises me when I hear this kind of view. We can only do the business by paying attention to the relationships. One of the precursors to doing business with anyone is to have rapport. Without rapport you have no basis for any kind of interaction. With rapport anything is possible.

As we saw in Chapter 10, rapport is the ability to join others where they are in order to create a climate of trust and respect. It is also important to be in rapport with yourself so that you are aligned with what you think, say, do, believe and stand for.

The only person who can build rapport is you. I was presenting this point to a manager who was having difficulty working with his boss. He asked me why he couldn't expect his boss to come half way and I replied that his boss wasn't there. If I had been talking to his boss about the same kind if issue, I would have made the same kind of point – that it was each person's responsibility to build rapport. You can only change yourself and in so doing you influence others around you. If you expect or wait for them to change you may wait for ever. Can you afford to do that? I suspect not. You lead by your example. What you give is what you get. By making the effort to build rapport, you encourage others to respond to you in the same way. This may not be immediately and with some people maybe not at all, but you can't afford not to find out.

The only person who can build rapport is you

You may find that some consultants and trainers advise you to build rapport by matching the body language of the person with whom you are dealing. I think this is superficial if it is used in isolation. Nevertheless, if someone is matching or following your behavior then it is an indicator that you have rapport.

In a team, you are more likely to be building rapport if you are matching the values of the other team members. This is why it is so useful to agree what the core values are for the team and those you believe to be key to the future of the business.

It would be unfair for me to publish the name of the company of which the team in the earlier case study was a part. Suffice it to say that it was the top team of a subsidiary company in an international bank. Its members decided to spend a weekend away to resolve how they might find a way to work together and even just stay in the same room long enough!

I facilitated this weekend. There was one piece of thinking that made the difference: I offered them the thinking that what they recognized in others was in fact a reflection of themselves and that by thinking this they could take ownership and therefore influence the effect they were having in the team. Because they were so stressed with how the team had not succeeded in working together up to that point, they seized on this way of thinking as a way forward. The results were immediate. They owned instead of blaming. They looked within instead of outside of themselves. We dealt with each member of the team in turn. There was no question in my mind that they were influenced by the managing director's openness to learn and to be open and vulnerable. The tension left the group and they enjoyed each other's company in all their discussions. Interestingly, they had always enjoyed each other's company socially and this was enhanced.

I received a call within a few days of the weekend to say that they had spent the Monday in a meeting together which had resulted in the production of their first ever business strategy. No one had left the meeting and they had totally cooperated with each other to resolve any differences they may have had.

PORTLAND HOLIDAYS

Portland Holidays is part of the Thomson Tour Operations Group. It conducts its business from a call center in Manchester, UK. Its original offices were destroyed by the bomb that blew apart a shopping and office area in the heart of the city a few years ago. It is so easy to hear of events such as this and not fully appreciate the lasting impact that they can have on people's lives and businesses. Although no one from Portland was hurt in that blast and although amazingly the company was up and running from an alternative site within 24 hours, staff are still experiencing the aftermath of that shock and disruption to the business.

Nevertheless, the managers of Portland have used this as an opportunity to stand back and take stock of how they do business and look at how they can lift their operations to a new level of expertise. The travel industry is possibly one of the most difficult in which to take this sort of action, given that it is such a reactive market and the competition is so great, with some of the smallest margins in any business.

This stock taking was helped by the appointment of a new manager who brought with him new ways of thinking and working, in particular a desire to introduce greater ownership, accountability and forward thinking. A number of stages led up to our work with the Portland management team, including some one-to-one sessions with the line manager.

The work with the management team involved:

- them exploring what they needed from each other
- them learning more about their individual styles so they could enhance the rapport they experienced as a team and develop relationships with which to talk through the most difficult issues, whatever they might be
- them clarifying their key result areas, i.e. the parts of the business for which they had unique accountability, so that everyone was clear about who was responsible for achieving which outputs in the business
- them developing their coaching skills so they could manage and facilitate their own development, but also the development of the staff who reported to them

In particular, the things that probably had the most significant effect on changes in thinking came as a result of the openness and willingness of the management team to step into and own such beliefs as:

- The meaning of the communication is the effect – they took ownership of the responses they got from others. For example, rather than saying 'Well, I emailed her' when one of the team members had not got a message about a key change, to say instead 'Well, that didn't work. How else can I be sure that she gets the messages

The meaning of the communication is the effect

I want to communicate to her?' And at another level, they learned to own the fact that the performance of their staff was the meaning (the direct effect) of the way they were managing them.

People have all the resources they need to achieve what they want

- People have all the resources they need to achieve what they want – which led to them involving others more in decision-making processes, rather than dictating to them as would have been the case in the past. This particular belief was the foundation for them adopting a coaching style of managing, recognizing that they and the people they managed had far more resources within themselves than had previously been utilized. They realized that now was the time to learn how to draw out those resources and use them in the business.

What was also important was how the team explored the thinking behind their thinking in relation to the key result areas within the business. They identified what they believed to be the core values of the business for the future and how they communicated those values. In particular, they identified the metamessages they were giving in what they chose to measure in their own and their staff's performance. For example, they had in the past measured time spent not on the phones – in the cloakrooms or away from desks. They had also measured numbers of calls referred to the management team because the staff had not been able to handle them. And although they were aiming for a decline in figures related to both, they were nevertheless measuring the problem states.

The consequence of measuring problems is more problems

Similar to 'what you think is what you get' in connection with performance measures, 'what you measure is what you get', even if you are measuring a decline. If you pay attention to the problems – in whatever way you do that – then problems are what you get. So the team shifted to measuring the key results that they did really want, as opposed to those that they didn't. This was a simple shift but a 180° turnaround in culture. The metamessage shifted from 'We don' t trust you – you need to be policed' to 'We trust you and we expect outstanding results from you and a focus on what matters to the success of the business.'

The influence we have on people around us and people who work with us is often unconscious. By becoming consciously aware of how they were giving messages to the people they managed as well as to each other, the members of this team began to choose to communicate messages of acceptance and trust and expectation of good performance. And of course, people responded to just those messages.

In one of the companies I worked with the culture was to work long hours and to sacrifice home life. There was always something else to be done, always a potential crisis to manage. This was interesting, as the company product was one that was to do with fun and freedom. I worked with various staff over a period of about six months. There were many choices about what areas to focus on for the training and we covered a lot and saw big changes in the way the staff worked and the results they achieved.

One of the challenges of being a consultant is to be sufficiently in rapport with the culture of the business to understand and influence it, but not so much as to become it. The ability to change your state at the end of a piece of work and resume your own style is key. We were at the end of a challenging day in which the team had had some major insights and shifts in their thinking. We had worked through issues for each team member respectively, but had not completed the work for everyone in the team. We were 20 minutes off the stated finish time and the proposal from the team was to work on for, say, an extra 20 minutes to complete the work for the remaining team members. It was tempting – there was a logic to this idea. Fortunately, I stepped back sufficiently from what was happening to have the realization to say 'no'. That was probably one of the most important contributions I made to that team – we finished on time!

THOUGHT PROVOKERS

1 Think of someone with whom you have contact and with whom you don't get on too well. Now ask yourself the questions: How is their reaction to you a direct result of how you act towards them and have acted in the past? For how long have you responded to each other in the way you do right now? How long might it take to reverse those responses to each other? Imagine for a moment how you might be if you were functioning as a team – what is that like? Until you can imagine it you cannot attain it, so allow yourself to wonder what it could be like even though you don't have that right now. What would it be like if that teamwork were enhanced even further, beyond your wildest dreams – what is that like?

2 Which of the presuppositions mentioned in the chapter do you think you fully hold and which do you think you would benefit from holding? Just to remind you, the presuppositions mentioned were:
   ● the map is not the territory
   ● people make the best choices available to them
   ● the meaning of the communication is the effect

3 What would be the implications for you of holding any presuppositions that you identified in the previous question? How might you and others benefit?

4 What are the teams to which you belong and what are the bigger teams to which you also belong that came into your thinking as you were reading the chapter? What is your contribution to those teams? Does your contribution differ from one team to another or is there a constant? If so, what is it?

5 How committed are you to meeting and supporting the needs of the other people in the teams of which you are a part? How long does your commitment last? Is it temporary or is it for a lifetime?

6 What steps have you taken to find out the needs of other people in the teams of which you are a part? What more could you do?

7 How much time do you set aside each week to invest in developing the relationships in the teams of which you are a part? How much time would you like to spend and how will you make that happen?

8 Think of the best team of which you have ever been a member. How do you imagine it? What is the quality of what you see, hear and feel?

9 Identify two people in your life – one who influenced you positively and one who influenced you negatively or with whom you felt you had to struggle to maintain your self-esteem and your capabilities. What were the metamessages that each gave you by how they acted towards you and how did they do this?

Personal Selling Skills 13

Our very lives depend on the ethics of strangers, and most of us are always strangers to other people.
> Bill Moyers, address, University of Texas at Austin
> Commencement, 1988

*T*RADITIONAL sales techniques have had their day. The objection-handling and closing techniques that once put the bread on the table, when transported to the developing world of relationships and partnerships, have the same effect as turning a hosepipe on to a fireworks display. Customers have developed in their expectations of what they want from representatives of the companies with which they deal, and they have become more sophisticated in the way they expect to do business. Equally, the business world has become increasingly competitive and there is rarely a place for a mere 'order taker'. A salesperson today has to be multiskilled in both the technical content of their work and interpersonal skills.

It is interesting to compare traditional selling techniques with NLP-based sales training. In a recent discussion about selling with a group of consultants, they explained that they had been trained to ask their prospective clients questions in a terrier-like way until the client disclosed the problems they experienced with the processes in their business. Sometimes this worked with great success; there were some people who were delighted to have an audience for their problems. As one leading human resources consultant once put it: 'Don't tell people your problems – 80 percent don't care and 20 percent are glad.' I would add to this and say that of the 80 percent who don't care, 50 percent were salespeople who had been trained in problem-centered questioning techniques! However, the technique does not always work. On one occasion the potential client said they were not prepared to answer these questions and, when the salesperson persisted (as they had been trained to do), the client asked them to finish their coffee and leave.

Technique-based selling is hit and miss

Techniques alone are a hit-and-miss approach to selling. There are some people with whom the techniques will be successful, either because they are ready to buy or because the particular technique used happens to fit with their style. But this is Russian roulette, as the consultants in the previous example discovered. It is the skill and thinking that generate the technique that count – the sensitivity to detect the customer's reactions to what you are doing and saying moment by moment, as well as your flexibility to adapt and do something else if what you are doing isn't working. The more choices you have, the more flexibility, the more routes you have to achieve an outcome that fits for you both.

CREATING A VISION

Contrast this with my experience in the Marlborough Oriental Rug Company. We called in on our way home from Westbury in Wiltshire, UK. It was the carpet in the window that had attracted us a few weeks earlier on the same return journey. The window display was changed often, so the carpet we liked was no longer on display. We were greeted informally by the owner and allowed to wander and browse. When we eventually asked him a question, we found ourselves drawn into conversation about exotic lands and journeys that were the homes of the beautiful carpets that were scattered around the shop. We shared stories of our travels and I am sure that we could have been there for hours past the official closing time if we had chosen to.

Eventually we got on to the subject of the carpet that had attracted us to the shop in the first place. We weren't sure if it would look right in our house, so he suggested without hesitation that we take it and try it and either send him a cheque if it did go with our furnishings or return it on our next time through. He did not know who we were or where we lived or when we would next be in Westbury. Here was a complete demonstration of trust. We took the carpet on this basis, were pleased with it and sent him the cheque. I would of course want to buy from him again. I value the trust he placed in us almost as much as the value he added to our whole experience of buying the carpet.

INTERNATIONAL COMPUTERS LTD

International Computers Ltd (ICL) has held its place in the world of mainframe manufacture and software development for the last 25 years and has seen many other similar organizations come and go. Even so, the company has taken some major steps forward in its thinking about its purpose and role today.

ICL's mission now is to:

'Design, build and operate systems and services which enable our customers to create, maintain and develop personal relationships with the people who use their products or services.'

The strategic objective that the company holds to fulfill this mission is 'to grow a global systems and services business in the Information Society'. It defines the Information Society as a world where people's lives are enriched by information services.

Consequently, the ability to build relationships and to promote the services and systems that are the company's products is key to the achievement of the goal. Therefore ICL decided to invest in ways to develop the relationship-building skills of its salesforce. For such a mission to succeed, the workforce of the company need to live out the values of the business in everything they do. This became one of the goals of the sales training program that we conducted.

THE OUTCOME OF THE PROJECT

The outcome of the project was improved results on the bottom line of the business. It is not unusual for me to come across the view that spending time developing relationships is not connected with the results of the business; that it is a luxury we invest in if we want to be seen to be doing the right thing. Consequently, challenging this belief is an essential ingredient of the program. There is no point ploughing ahead with some of the new ways of thinking if the fundamental belief that supports these ways of thinking is not yet in place.

NOT JUST A SOCIAL CHAT

The ability to build rapport was one of the themes of the program. We had an interesting reaction to this. Many of the salespeople thought that building rapport was about chatting about the weather, asking about the other person's family or just socializing. 'Build rapport' was even one of the items at the top of a sales call checklist, although some said they didn't always have time for this.

The program showed them how building rapport meant matching the client wherever they were in style, in interests, in values, in expectations...

In one case, a salesperson entered the office of one of a client's senior decision makers to be greeted with someone who was abrupt, pushing for a fast response, direct to the point of aggression and intolerant of 'fools'! To have started talking about the weather or the photos on the wall would not have been taken too well, as you might imagine. In this instance rapport, at least initially, was to speak quickly, to get to the point without delay, to use the time effectively and to ensure that the salesperson checked they were doing so by making absolutely sure they understood what this manager wanted out of the 45 minutes he had allocated for the meeting. It was not necessary to be aggressive, but it was appropriate to match the firmness of the aggression with a certainty of presentation and view.

In essence, what ICL is doing for its salesforce through NLP-based programs is building on the considerable expertise that they already have by:

ENHANCING EXISTING
EXPERIENCE

- developing their sensitivity to the verbal and nonverbal signs that their customers give out
- increasing their flexibility by not only making them aware of the styles they already use but by giving them new choices in both what they think and in what they do
- creating an openness in their receptivity to feedback about how they are being received by the people with whom they deal, not only their customers but their colleagues, their managers, their partners in life
- building a set of beliefs that support them in taking total responsibility for the results they get and the experience they have with all the people with whom they come into contact
- enhance their skill in building instantaneous and lasting rapport with their contacts

And the result...

'This program has been a **win** at an individual, at the program level and at the level of the operating division. It is like a food cycle. By supporting each other each individual is supporting themselves and by the very nature of this they are supporting the community. The people who have gone through this program have become a community.

I genuinely believe that this program has delivered **real value**. NLP-based training of this form is not about having bolt-on goodies *and it is not about just what happens to be the flavor of the day. Programs that have these characteristics fall into disrepute as a result. This is 'real' and is seeking to add further colors and definition to existing skills because it is targeted at the individual. It is as such a form of Micro Marketing. It is broad in its remit but it is a rifle shot. It is not prescriptive; it is something different to each person on the program. Each person takes away something very personal.*

We have each fed off the input and fed off each other to the betterment of the whole. We have all achieved individual wins.

And personally, I have always believed that if I live my life on my own terms I cannot further my development within a bigger organization. By focusing on my self-belief I am enthused to believe that I can have and do both.'

David Sinclair, ICL Client Director

UNISYS

At the time of writing this chapter, there is an advertisement in the *Sunday Times* for Unisys. The main caption reads:

'Unisys knows it takes two things to run a successful business. One of them is people.'

This is exactly what our sales training programs at the company were designed to achieve – an emphasis on people. Other Unisys key phrases are:

- Making every client contact count
- Building solutions
- Understanding needs
- Client dedicated

In the company's words:

'We are one of the world's largest information service providers. We design, build, and integrate information management solutions that help clients in selected market sectors attract and retain customers and improve their competitiveness.'

To do this, it is crucial that the Unisys people who have contact with customers have not only the technical skills to design the solutions, but also the interpersonal skills to balance the technicalities with the ability to relate to people needs.

Although the emphasis that Unisys wanted to put on this new program was personal selling skills, it was evident that this was not only relevant to the salesforce but to anyone who had contact with customers. In reality, the project managers had the most lasting contact with customers and also had to have the skill to manage a team of technical people to relate to the needs of the customer.

'Our traditional sales training has placed a lot of emphasis on techniques. I was much more interested in relationships and how successful salespeople are able to build and maintain excellent relationships with their clients to the extent that the client wants to do business with them.

My own experience, on the receiving end of sales calls, is that it is very obvious when a salesperson is using techniques without the sensitivity to their own or others' feelings, values or beliefs. When that happens I feel much more like an object than a person. I prefer, and find it much easier, to do business with people who are able to relate to me and empathize with my feelings and needs.

This begs the question, how do you do empathy? Traditional sales training suggests that you begin a sales meeting by building rapport. But how do you do that? In fact, our consultants and project managers are "doing" rapport most of the time, but without being consciously aware of what they do. I was keen to have the kind of training which would enable them to recognize what works well for them, and to apply it consciously and systematically in their dealings with clients.

It was also clear to me that many of our consultants and project managers were uncomfortable with the notion of being a salesperson. The phrase "I don't see myself as a salesperson" can often be heard. Equally clear, though, is that these same people frequently have very well-developed influencing skills.

So another goal of the training was to help people become more aligned and comfortable with the role of "influencer", and how they

I WANTED TO BUY FROM HER

can influence others in a way that is in alignment with their own ethics, values and beliefs.'

Rob Mottram, Training Manager, Unisys

Unisys ran a series of two-day sales programs with a follow-up day two months later to review the experiences of the delegates. It also offered one-day introductions to the new thinking so that those people who were interested in knowing what it was all about could come along and find out for themselves in the company of many others in the same position.

The two-day program exposed the delegates to two guests who were both successful salespeople but with subtle differences in their style. One was more inclined to 'sell' and the other more oriented towards 'building relationships'. Both impressed the groups, but the reactions were interestingly different:

'He sold to me ... but I wanted to buy from her.'

The aim of the Unisys programs was to increase the former but to balance it with more of the latter.

THE DIFFICULT CUSTOMER

The projects that Unisys engages in are often large and complex, and frequently involve not only technical solutions but also reengineering of business processes.

A typical example in the banking sector would be reengineering of a bank's branch operations. A project to introduce new ways of working across possibly hundreds of branches will affect staff at every level in the client organization – from the board to the frontline counter staff in the branch.

Unisys consultants and project managers, as well as salespeople, need to manage a number of different factors, not the least of these being the different and often conflicting needs and expectations of people throughout the customer's organization. This is one of the main areas that Unisys has addressed with its training: understanding the client's world, what's important to them, what motivates them, and being able to communicate with them in ways that match their experience. Inevitably, this means that there are many different factors to manage, including the customer and their unique expectations.

When there is so much going on, it can be tempting to think of the customer and their changing needs as 'difficult'. And if, for example, you think of your customer as difficult, no amount of massaging of your behavior on the surface will conceal that thought from leaking out, even in the most minimal of ways.

Unisys is helping its salesforce to manage themselves so that they have the resources to think of each of their customers as special.

What you think is what you communicate.

What you think is what you communicate

With such an emphasis and strength in the ability to provide technical solutions, Unisys recognized the need to address the imbalance with people skills. Not only does the customer buy your ability to provide a solution, but more than that they buy you. The question then arises: 'Are you adding value by being who you are?' What most influences the way you are in any situation is your state. Take stock for a moment: what is your state as you read these words? Are you curious about how you can apply these ideas? Are you tense because you have other things to do or other things on your mind? Are you relaxed, because reading is something you do when you have plenty of time? Are you motivated and compelled, as you want to learn to enhance your personal and business success? It may be some, none or all of these, but you have some state and that influences everything you do.

This is what Unisys recognized – the importance of managing a person's individual state so that they had one that would enhance meetings with their clients. They did this in many ways, which included challenging their presuppositions regarding the clients they dealt with, setting compelling outcomes for themselves, putting themselves in their clients' shoes and more.

THE CUSTOMER BUYS YOU

The salesman entered the potential client's office. In accordance with his training, he looked around the walls for inspiration for a topic with which to build rapport. The walls were lined with photographs of dogs, so he proceeded to make conversation about dogs for the next 10 minutes.

The potential client, who had been looking increasingly puzzled, eventually stopped him and asked: 'Why are you spending so much time talking about dogs?'

The salesperson replied: 'Well, I noticed that you were interested in dogs from all the pictures that you have on the wall.'

'But this isn't my office,' the potential client replied. He remains a potential client to this day.

THOUGHT PROVOKERS

1   Identify the last three successful sales calls that you
    made and the last three unsuccessful ones. Take yourself
    back in your thinking to the moments before you
    engaged with your client. What was your state in each?
    Give each state a name and describe the exact qualities
    of what you were feeling, i.e. what kind of feeling, where
    you felt it, what qualities it had. What patterns do you
    notice between the ones in which you were successful
    and the ones in which you weren't successful? Choose
    the state that you feel is most conducive to your next
    sales situation. Plan how you will recreate this state for
    yourself. One of the easiest ways is to fully associate into
    the time when you had it most strongly before.

2   Identify the client with whom you would most like to build
    rapport, the one with whom you feel you have the most
    scope to build a better relationship. Identify what is
    different about their style, interests, needs, values and
    behavior in relation to yours. Choose some of these
    elements that you haven't matched before or haven't
    matched successfully. Plan how you will do this on the
    next contact that you have with them.

3   Pick one client with whom you would like to increase
    your effectiveness, particularly someone who seems to
    misunderstand your actions or your intentions. Imagine a
    typical situation that you would be in with this client, one
    where there have been misunderstandings in the past or
    may even still be present today. Imagine yourself with
    them and first of all put yourself in your shoes, looking
    and listening and feeling what you feel with them. Now
    step back so that you are just behind yourself in the way
    that you are imagining the situation. What are the
    messages that you are giving out in the way you are
    doing what you are doing, i.e. what are the
    metamessages? If you are not sure, look and listen to
    the response that you are getting from your client. What
    are they responding to? How are these true in the way

you are behaving? What messages would you like to be
giving out instead? What will you change in what you
are thinking or doing or the way in which you are doing
it that will communicate these different messages?

Exceptional Tutoring 14

My preaching at its best had itself been personal counselling on a group scale.

    Harry Emerson Fosdick, *The Living of These Days*, 1956

*T*o consult the best you must be the best. Top consultants need to combine excellence in technical and project management skills with the most sensitive and enabling people-handling skills – a rare combination. And to coach those top consultants requires people who are a model of excellence in all that they promote: they need to be skilled in challenging those they coach to reach a potential that even they might not have dreamed would be possible.

This was the challenge facing PricewaterhouseCoopers, one of the top financial consultancies in the world, in exploring how its consultants could consistently achieve the levels of excellence needed to do the work they do through their consultant tutors.

Their consultant tutors have responsibility for coaching and training the consultants in the rest of the company worldwide. What PricewaterhouseCoopers wanted was to be able to identify what makes an excellent tutor working in the contexts that they do. Whatever means of measurement you use, there are a few tutors who excel in this role. These are the people who have the respect of the staff they train, they are the ones who get consistently top marks in the student feedback ratings, and they are the ones who consistently coach others to reach standards of work that they have not previously realized. These top tutors are the ones who time and time again bring out the best in the best.

They bring out the best in the best

TO MODEL THE BEST

The contact in PricewaterhouseCoopers went straight to the heart of NLP in deciding what they wanted from this work. They wanted to model the best of their consultant tutors to identify the conscious and unconscious strategies that constitute the difference that makes the difference between those who excel and the rest. Given the standards in PricewaterhouseCoopers, the rest achieve a level of excellence in what they do of which most people in similar roles in other professions would be proud. So what we were looking for here was the gold dust on the top of the treasure chest. And what PricewaterhouseCoopers wanted was for this difference to be made available to every consultant tutor so that this exceptional standard of performance could be achieved by all.

It was not as if they were without training and awareness of what they did and how they did it. The consultant tutors were very aware and sensitive people with tremendous knowledge of what they did and what impact their actions had on others. This sensitivity to the effect of their behavior on others is a vital skill in the way they work. Nevertheless, they recognized that there were aspects of what they did that they did not consciously know and could not therefore teach to new consultant tutors. It was this that they wanted, as well as learning more about NLP in the process.

THE FRAME FOR THE MODELING

The PricewaterhouseCoopers tutors met for a conference each year and it was with this conference in mind that we planned the work. This annual event was an opportunity to present the conclusions of the work to all the tutors from around the world. Prior to that, we had the opportunity to see some of these top people in action running training events. Those who were based in other countries were available by phone or e-mail.

It is crucial that as part of the modeling process we see and hear the subjects in action. It is what they do, not what they think they do, that counts in modeling. If the answer lay in what they think they do they wouldn't need to model the process; they would have it already.

We therefore decided to use a framework for the modeling that would also lend itself to presentation at the conference. On this basis, we chose the logical levels of change (this was introduced on page 88). This was initially the basis for the questions to which I wanted answers in order to build a profile of the top tutors.

What I was curious about at each of the levels was the following:

ENVIRONMENT

- How did the tutors organize their environment, in particular the training room?
- How did the tutors manage their environment throughout the training and coaching sessions?
- What did they attribute to being outside of themselves (i.e. in their environment in the metaphorical sense)?
- What was the typical environment in which they worked and how was that a reflection of who they are as people?

BEHAVIOR

- What did they do and what did they say that was characteristic of the kind of person they are?
- What patterns were there in their behavior that were true for different tutors?
- What effect did their behavior have on the people with whom they came into contact and with whom they

worked? What effect did their behavior have on me in my dealings with them? (I found this to be a particularly valuable source of information.)

CAPABILITIES

- How do they do what they do, i.e. with what skills and qualities?
- What were their strategies for getting the results they got, whatever they were?
- What were the qualities that they demonstrated not only in the context of the training sessions they gave but also in any other context?
- What qualities and strategies did they employ in any of the communication that we had doing the modeling research?

VALUES

- What was important to them in life and in work?
- What was important to them in the interactions they had with the participants on their program?
- What did they say were their values and what did they demonstrate to be their values through their actions?

BELIEFS

- What were their beliefs? About themselves, others, work, life…?

IDENTITY

- What kind of person were they?
- What labels did they give themselves?
- What representation did they have of themselves?

PURPOSE

- What bigger systems did they consider themselves to be connected to?
- What added value did they seek to bring to these bigger systems?
- What was the purpose of what they did?
- What legacy did they want to leave with what they did?

These were the questions that were to form the basis and the backdrop to any conversations we had and to any of the observing I did of them in action. Not all of the questions are unique; some are variations on others and come at the same point from a slightly different direction. Not all questions were asked or answered, but they formed part of the original plan.

I was also curious about what the tutors understood this modeling exercise to be about. One of my first questions to them was what they thought made an excellent PricewaterhouseCoopers tutor. The replies included:

- It means having the participants walk out of the room having made some new connection or gained some new insight and knowing that I was a part of this process.
- It means having been able to deal with all the PricewaterhouseCoopers-related issues that come up on the course and to enable the delegates to gain new insights about them which they can put into practice in a way that means that they achieve results more effectively than before.
- It means having my content, delivery and materials set a new standard.
- It means enhancing skills that make a difference to the business's bottom line.

IN ESSENCE

In a world of problems and task-centered processes there is a need for people who can facilitate the thinking and skills that harness and release the true talents of and motivations of the people affected by the change. The excellent PricewaterhouseCoopers tutor has people skills in abundance and they manifest this in everything they do. They bring a balance with their excess of care, sensitivity and learning skills to the extreme task-oriented environment of change integration. Their people-centered skills and the respect they have for people in general exist in every aspect of their lives. They are congruent in their demonstration of these in their approach to work and home life and in the way they approach people in their courses, as well as the way they deal with anyone with whom they come into contact.

I have to be honest and say that what I discovered was a surprise to me. This is the delight in modeling and to me this proves that it is an objective process. I had had few dealings with PricewaterhouseCoopers previously and knew them from their reputation of years earlier. The catchphrase that summarized my secondhand impression was 'arrogant and proud of it'. How wrong I was and I was delighted to be proved wrong.

WHAT WE FOUND

An excellent PricewaterhouseCoopers tutor is one who does the following at each level:

ENVIRONMENT

- Organizes the environment to appeal to all senses, e.g. they have materials that appeal to the visual sense, when the training room is set up they have a display of visual material and very early on in the program the participants are invited to add to this. They appeal to the auditory sense by having music playing throughout all the breaks and as an introduction to some of the topics. They include activities throughout the program that involve the participants moving, doing and touching so the sense of touch and feeling is catered for throughout.

BEHAVIOR

- Uses metaphors that support and illustrate the culture they want to create, e.g. open doors, climbing mountains, the branches of a tree. Typically, the metaphors reflect language that is to do with the emerging values of the company, such as growth, openness, learning and challenge.
- Uses language that instructs participants' unconscious thinking in the direction of the course objectives. For example, a sentence of the form 'We would now like you to decide how you will identify some new strategies for growth' contains the command to the unconscious mind to 'decide'. This sentence would influence the participants to make decisions. This

would be in contrast with a sentence of the form: 'Don't worry about some of the resistance you might experience when you put your ideas forward.' Although the instruction is not to worry about the resistance, our unconscious minds do not recognize 'Don't' and so in this example the sentence invites the listener to 'worry about the resistance'.

- Match the participants' behavior, language and expectations and current thinking as a way of building rapport.
- Match the behavior and language of their co-tutors in a way that nonverbally communicates support.
- Model the behavior they want from the participants, e.g. if they want people to build rapport with each other they would do this in the way they relate to them. Essentially, they would be an example of what they are teaching. This is one of the most potent forms of influence there is.
- They would engage the participants' feelings by associating themselves and the participants into the learning experience and working real time on their issues with them, as opposed to presenting ideas purely as a theoretical model.
- Add value by bringing what they have to give in terms of their personal talents to course content/design.
- Have a strong negative reaction if someone they were working with did not understand or grasp a point they were making. This negative feeling would be even stronger if the participant did not like and expressed their dislike of what they were doing. Inevitably, with these top people this was not a usual occurrence, but it was so strong that they had coded it as one to be avoided at all cost.

CAPABILITIES

- Add value 'real time' by always using here and now opportunities to coach the participants.
- Build instantaneous rapport whatever the situation or the circumstances and whoever the person.
- Are constructive and positive in the way they give

feedback. They encourage regular and instant feedback in all they do.

- Are predominantly 'desired state' in their thinking and in their style of presentation, even though they have the ability to use problem-centered thinking and styles as a means of building rapport.
- Are continuously learning in their approach to what they do by making connections in what they experience, and as such are a congruent example of what they seek to bring about in the business.
- Have the skill to monitor what they are doing as they do it. Effectively, they can multitask.
- Are willing to take risks in what they do. So, for example, they will try a new approach in their interactions with their participants.
- Use enriched language (words that engage all senses) in the way they present.
- Have precision in their ability to calibrate body language.
- Are able to put themselves in other people's shoes and experience situations as if they were them. Consequently, they are able to present their ideas and thoughts in a way that fits for the state of the person or people with whom they are dealing.
- Are sensitive to energy levels – others' as well as their own.
- Are flexible and capable of improvization.
- Have systems thinking as the base of the way they operate with others, in that they identify totally with the person with whom they are dealing and act as if they are one system, totally synchronized with each other.

BELIEFS AND VALUES

- Have respect for others, both in the way they think and the way they behave towards others.
- Care for others – their colleagues, their families, and the whole human race.
- Are committed to the company's goals and to the ways in which they can progress those goals.

- Are committed to their own personal goals and to the progression of their career.
- Are able to learn and make constant improvements and challenge so they are stretched in their ability to do what they do.
- Are honest in what they say and what they do.
- Are able to change in finding new ways to do what they do.

- Have the identity of co-learner, guide, role model, teacher and servant.

IDENTITY

- Aim to help people realize their true talents.
- Want to improve the quality of life for all.

PURPOSE

In participating in this project, the tutors who were identified as the models of excellence became more aware and appreciative of the skills and attitudes that made them so special. Overall, their success was a measure of the alignment between their personal and work goals. They demonstrated this alignment in everything they did and in all the situations where I encountered them.

A few years ago I read a newspaper article describing the behavior of a schoolboy who had become so unruly that the teachers were recommending that the headteacher expel him. The boy bullied other children, swore at teachers and was usually involved in a fight at least a couple of times a week. The teachers had tried every form of punishment and detention that they could think of but the boy would not conform.

Eventually, the headteacher summoned him to his office. He gave the boy an ultimatum: 'You have this choice – either you accept the offer that I am about to explain to you or you will be expelled.' The boy said nothing.

The headmaster proceeded: 'This is the offer. Agree to the following or you will be expelled. You are to agree to bully once a week, to swear a total of five times a day (this was a lot less than the current behavior) and to fight once.'

This approach on the part of the headmaster was heavily criticized in the press – but he was trying to get the boy to obey at least one set of rules.

THOUGHT PROVOKERS

Consider a goal that you would like to achieve – something that is important to you. It could be a goal that you have had for some time but have never found a way to achieve. Think about your goal alongside each of following questions:

1 How would achieving this goal be supported by people around you in your work and in your life?
2 What resources can you draw on to achieve this goal?
3 What would you be doing when you have achieved this goal?
4 What skills would you be using in achieving this goal?
5 What skills would you be releasing in achieving this goal?
6 How would achieving this goal fulfill your core values?
7 What can you believe that will support you in the achievement of the goal?
8 How does achieving this goal fit with the person you truly are?
9 How does achieving this goal contribute to your higher purpose?
10 How has your goal evolved as you have been answering these questions and how would you now like it to evolve?

15 *High-performance Coaching*

Man cannot live without a permanent trust in something indestructible in himself, though both the indestructible element and the trust may remain permanently hidden from him.

Franz Kafka, *Reflections*

'WE don't want any of that personal development!' These were the words of an HR manager in an international organization. That company is not faring too well in these days of flattened structures, increased accountability and the need for continuous learning.

The patterns of thinking and acting on the part of most senior people set the trend for the culture of that organization. If the active leader thrives on conflict, then so will the company – although the rest of the staff may not have the skills to deal with the conflict. If the leader is caring and compassionate, then it is likely that this will be the style that ripples through the organization and out to its customers. The leader of a business is constantly coaching those around them by every action they take moment by moment, day by day. We coach by our example.

And so it follows that the development of these leaders is key to the success and growth of the business. It is their ability to learn that will influence the learning culture of the rest of the organization. Equally, it is their inhibitions about learning that will, in the same way, limit the company's capability. So it is crucial that these leaders examine who they are and what their example is to others.

Standard training programs typically do not meet this need. There is often no time for the individual attention that is needed to identify the conscious and unconscious patterns that make us who we are. And so often the pressures on the time of a chief executive or managing director make it difficult for them to give time to a dedicated course. So more and more of these senior people are turning to personal coaching sessions, one-to-one sessions with a skilled facilitator who can support, challenge, feedback and coach them to be the example they truly want to be for themselves and for the future of the business. It is lonely at the top, but rather than just find company these leaders need mentors and personal coaches who will be the friend that will tell and ask them what others may not.

Lonely at the top

HOW DOES NLP MAKE A DIFFERENCE?

There are many excellent books and consultants teaching coaching skills, so what is the difference in an approach that uses NLP as its base? The key to the answer lies at the heart of NLP.

As I have said throughout this book, NLP is the process of modeling 'the difference that makes the difference'. It is a process of benchmarking the conscious and especially the unconscious processes that enable us to achieve the results we do, good or bad. Whatever our experience and whatever results we achieve, we have a sequence of thinking and behavior patterns that form our strategy (our program) for achieving exactly this.

If you have the ability to present your ideas to your staff in a way that is compelling, you have a way of preparing your thoughts and materials that makes this possible. But you also have a pattern of thoughts and actions that may be so swift that you take them for granted and these are also part of how you prepare yourself to do this. There may be some subtleties in your language of which you are unaware that make your presentations as compelling as they are.

If you create panic, you have a strategy for doing this

If, however, you have the ability to create panic and crisis around you, then you also have a strategy by which you do this. I don't mean that you do this intentionally (although there may be some people who do), but unconsciously you think and act in a habitual way that has this effect.

We are all an integral part of a bigger system, which means that whatever the status of this bigger system we are a vital part of what makes it what it is. So NLP offers ways of discovering what we do that creates these results. The effect of knowing how we do what we do means that we have choice: choice to do more of the same or choice to do differently. The mere fact of becoming aware of what we do and how we do it is an integral part of the coaching process. So to model is to coach, or at least to provide the window of opportunity to make some new choices.

'A MAN WITH A MISSION'

It was Graham's wife who made the first contact. She played an operational role in her husband's business and she was concerned about the level of anxiety her husband was experiencing to do with all aspects of his work. So Graham decided, on her advice, to go for one-to-one coaching for himself and the business. Needless to say, the business had lost direction and it was losing many pitches for new business in which it knew it could have succeeded if the people involved had presented themselves with confidence. Graham was no longer enjoying the work and was experiencing sleepless nights. He looked very tired when we met.

We had an initial one-to-one conversation to establish what it was that he wanted. During this conversation, I noticed that he did not use 'I' in his vocabulary, and when he talked about either his personal or his business goals he talked about what he didn't want or what he wanted to change in some way. His attention, in both his conversation and his inner dialogue, was primarily problem centered. He paid attention to what was wrong, what might go wrong or what he didn't want to do.

When I pointed out that he didn't say 'I', he explained that he had played down his own needs for the last year since realizing that his natural style was to dominate his management team. Increasingly, he had dismissed his own wants to the point where, without realizing it, he had eliminated 'I' from his language. Needless to say, in meetings with clients he now felt that he was insufficiently important to deal with them and he found himself increasingly unable to manage his reactions to them, especially when he was challenged.

We met on a monthly basis and by our third meeting Graham was able to articulate what he really wanted. This was to take much more of a back seat in the current business and to set up a new company that allowed him to use the creativity and vision that he had stifled for so long. However, he had not allowed himself time to explore in his thinking how this might be. He felt he still lacked the self-esteem to plan how he might achieve this.

One of the presuppositions that was discovered in the early days of modeling with NLP is that those people who achieve what they want believe that they have all the resources within themselves to achieve it. The key is to tap into those resources. This same belief is also one that is held by those coaches who have the ability to enable the people that they coach to discover those lost or hidden resources. So with Graham the question was, where was his self-esteem? He had undoubtedly had self-esteem in the past to build the original business in the way that he had. Where was it to be found now?

The key is to tap into all our resources

I asked him if he would be prepared to allow himself the time now to explore what it might be like to have this new company that he so wanted to form. He agreed and

he stepped into the future to imagine what it was like to have it. He was immediately able to see the building and the people working within it. He could hear the sounds of the machines working and the buzz of excitement in the staff's voices. He could smell what it was like to be there and he felt the warmth of the air.

And then he explored what it was like emotionally to be there. He felt good about himself, at peace and satisfied. Here was his self-esteem! Although he had felt this self-esteem in the past, it was now to be found in the future vision. And the interesting thing about the future is that by imagining what it is like to have it, we have its qualities and the feelings about it today. By allowing himself the time to explore his vision for the future, Graham found the self-esteem that he wanted in order to manage his gradual exit from the mainstream business and to find a successor. He also found the state within himself to make the future dream a reality.

THE KEY TO HIGH-PERFORMANCE COACHING

What we can offer through nondirectional coaching are the high-quality feedback and questions that are so often missing, especially from the everyday lives of some senior managers. They may appraise others, although even then appraisals so often take the form of a prescriptive monologue – but who appraises the most senior manager? Who dares? And even for those who do, who has the skill to tell them what they need to hear in a way that they can hear it? Once the most senior people have experienced and learned this approach, they can then model it for the rest of the organization.

So what was going on for Graham in our preceding example? As I noted above, modeling his patterns in speech and behavior I noticed that he did not use 'I' in his vocabulary. Patterns in speech are the surface indicators of how we make sense of our experience and run deep in terms of how we make meaning of our lives. Graham had deleted 'I' from his speech. Deletion is one of the ways by which we change our experience. The key question is whether what we are doing works for us. This pattern had

worked for Graham, in that he had used it as a way to
make himself less aggressive in his style, which is what he
had recognized in himself some time before. But now it
was working against him in that he felt his significance was
less than that of others, especially in sales meetings. It was
also working against him in that he had lost connection
with his vision.

To feel compelled by a vision it is important to be able
to step into it and experience and feel it as if you have it.
Part of this is being able to fully experience 'I'. Equally, to
feel on a par with others you need to have a
representation of yourself as in balance with them. Balance
can show itself in many ways, one of these being the
balance between the references to yourself and others in
conversation – 'I' and 'me' related to 'them' and 'you'.

Graham also used 'away from' language, in that he
would be more likely to talk about what he didn't want or
what he had or ought to do, as opposed to what he really
wanted to do or what he could do. On the basis that what
we think is what we get, what Graham was getting was a lot
of what he didn't want or what he felt he ought to have.
This, not surprisingly, meant that he was often in a state of
anxiety or tension. 'Oughts' and 'musts' and 'don't wants'
typically associate with a physically tense state or a state
of anxiety.

Modeling these patterns that Graham was unconsciously
using meant that we brought to conscious awareness the
structure of his experience, i.e. how he was programming
himself to get the results he was getting. Once he had this
feedback, he had to choose consciously either to continue
to run the patterns or to make some new choices. His new
choices (which did not eliminate the old ones, merely
added to them) included the choice to use 'I' and as a
result to balance the way he thought about himself with the
way he thought about others. Another choice was to begin
to allow time to explore what he really did want and to
develop what that looked, sounded and felt like.

The combination of these new choices led to an
increase in self-esteem for Graham and to his sharing his

vision with the rest of his company. Once he had begun to express his vision, others were able to react to it and to look to how they could support him in achieving it.

NONDIRECTIONAL COACHING

I offered Graham neither advice nor any ready-made solutions. So often, the natural response to someone with a problem or a question is to tell them what to do. 'You know what you should do...' 'If I were you I would...' 'What I did when I was in similar situation was...' or, probably even worse, 'You think you've got problems – you should come and work in my department!' This is not to say that these sorts of responses don't have a place, they do. The problem arises when we only have the choice of responding in this way. If we want to coach ourselves or those around us, then to give a ready-made answer is to do what we have done before. And if we do what we have always done we will get what we always got. In the business world we need new, smarter, innovative ways of moving forward into the future.

If we do what we always did we'll get what we always got

If we prescribe solutions to others, we convey the metamessage that they don't have the resources within themselves to achieve what they want. If we facilitate and coach in a nondirectional way, then we communicate at this higher level that we do believe they have the resources within them to achieve what they want. This is what high-performance coaching is all about and it is at the heart of a learning culture. By providing the space for others to find their true resources, we encourage them to release their true potential and to use it to uncover a solution that is unique to who they are and that has their full commitment – because it is theirs.

A CAREER CONFLICT

Tim had inferred on a number of occasions that he was facing a big decision in his life. An opportunity arose for us to spend some time together when we could discuss this. He first broached the subject broadly and then began to describe a conflict he was experiencing regarding the next step in his career. He was in conflict with the part of himself that wanted to move on and to take a big step up in the kind of role that he fullfilled. This new step would involve him at least doubling his salary, but would also mean leaving the UK and working in the US. He was torn between taking this move and his wish to stay with the team that he had built up in his current role – a team that was working well together and growing.

As he described his present situation, he moved his left hand whereas his right hand remained static. When he referred to the future role that he was considering, it was his right hand that moved and the left one lay still on his lap.

This description of his situation suggested the use of a classic NLP format – conflict integration – which involves treating those aspects of yourself that are in conflict as separate parts and exploring how those parts can work together and become an integrated part of yourself with a completely new way of thinking that offers a way forward that meets all the needs.

I asked Tim first to describe the part of himself that wanted to stay with the team that he had built in the UK. I invited him to imagine that this part of himself was in his left hand, so that he could disconnect from the emotions of it for the time being. He became quite still and his voice slowed as he described this part as one that was concerned with relationships and that took pleasure in its achievements. He smiled and made steady eye contact. He said that this was the part of himself that was content with what he had and that could enjoy the present.

I invited him now to consider the other part – the one that was represented in his right hand. (It is no coincidence that we say things like: 'On the one hand I wanted this but then on the other hand…') He started to move and to breathe in a shallower way. He described this part of himself as the ambitious part – the part that pushed ahead and thought about the future. He spoke quickly as he described these qualities.

I invited him now to stand back and consider what both

parts wanted for him, i.e. what their common purpose was. He answered immediately, saying that they both wanted him to enjoy his work and his life and both wanted him to learn from whatever happened to him. I asked him to say what each part valued in the other, and he replied that the part that wanted to stay with the team really admired the ambition of the other part, and that part in turn admired the loyalty of the first part to people and to the relationships that it had. I asked him to invite the parts to accept these 'gifts' of the qualities that they admired in each other as if they were their own. As he did this, his hands came together and he automatically brought them to his chest. After a few moments, he sighed and smiled and said he could see a way forward now. I don't know what conclusion he came to (I could guess), but he was relaxed and quiet.

There was more detail to what we did in the discussion, but this summarizes some of the key elements. What was interesting was that I had noticed the characteristics of these two parts earlier in our discussions. Sometimes Tim had the ability to be very focused on what was happening in the present and gave exquisite attention to what people around him were saying and doing. He was at these times a very skilled modeler and he explained that that was how he had developed his skill in one of the sports he loved, by watching attentively someone who was excellent and whom he admired. Then at other times he changed state completely and began to move a lot in his chair and play with his watch. At these times he disconnected from the people he was with and usually made a comment about the time. This was when his attention was entirely on the future. Of course, both states were useful to him.

How we can release a new potential

These formats for change are about how we can get our inner resources to work in harmony, as opposed to being in conflict, and how by doing this we can release a new potential that uses our combined talents. Our patterns and our conflicts exist at all times and in many different contexts until we resolve them. They are not peculiar to just one decision, as Tim demonstrated.

A state of rapport with yourself comes from having all parts working in harmony. The same is true for a team or for a company, but it starts with yourself. When you are in rapport with yourself, you are at your most effective and it is then that you are in a position to give what you most have to give to your work, your team, your company, your family, your friends, your life. This parts approach to conflict resolution is one way to achieve that state.

ONLY WORDS

I love the linguistics element of NLP. Business depends on language more than ever before, especially with the rise of service industries, the importance of customer satisfaction and the dramatic increase in call centers where business is done over the phone.

During a workshop I was exploring the goals of the delegates. One of them, Grant, had a compelling goal for himself which he had wanted for many years. This goal was characterized by the image of a house with bluebell-carpeted woodland. He wanted to own a wood. He also had a sense that he had within him an untapped oil well, which would gush forth once he had found the key to his growth.

Grant had recently joined the department and the role was a new one for him, so he was keen to seize the opportunity to develop his potential and there was no doubt in my mind that he had the potential to excel at this kind of work. However, he identified that although he had this compelling goal he did not know how to achieve it; he did not know what the milestones were along the way. The conversation went as follows:

Me   *'What are those milestones?'*
Grant   *'I need to think about what they are.'*
Me   *'How about you think about them now?'*
Grant   *'Now?'* (I nodded.) *'Well, the only sense I have of what they might be is that I need to build up a network of contacts*

within the business and that I need to develop teambuilding events.'

Me   'What sorts of contacts?'

Grant   'I don't know'. (He leaned back and looked up.)

Me   'Who might be the kinds of people that you think you might want to contact?'

Grant   'Well, I suppose decision makers.'

Me   'And how can you contact them?'

Grant   'I'm not sure. I'll have to give some thought to that.'

Me   'How about you give some thought to it now?'

Grant   'I feel really challenged and uncomfortable.'

Me   'What would you like?'

Grant   'Well, I'm trying to think how I would remember these steps. I think I need to write them down.'

Me   'So...'

Grant   'I need to think...'

Me   'How would you like to do that?'

Grant   'I suppose I want some time to write my thoughts down and I need to ask for help from other members of the team.'

Me   'How can you make that happen?'

Grant   'I guess I need to ask them.'

Me   'How can you do that?' (The other team members were there.)

Grant   'Just ask them, I guess.'

Me   'Well...'

Grant turned to the team members and asked them if they would arrange for him to meet some of the key decision makers in the parts of the business with which they each had contact. They immediately agreed.

What we discovered with this exchange and with others that had gone before was that Grant was very skilled at identifying the goals and the dreams, but less skilled at defining the steps to reach them. When asked for steps he usually expressed them in nonspecific ways or said that he needed time to think. Even when questioned, he would usually respond with another nonspecific action. Over and over again, the other team members and I would ask Grant: 'How will you do that?' He then began to ask this question for himself and developed the plans he did have in his thinking so that they were precise.

Grant made many connections with this session and events of the past. He recognized how when his father had died (whom he identified as being the doer of the family) he had offered his mother help in the business and had many goals that he had shared with her, but very few if any of them had materialized. He began to recognize similar patterns within himself as he had recognized in his mother. He started to catch himself when he gave a nonspecific answer and began automatically to ask himself: 'How can I do this now?'

This time with Grant highlighted for me the importance and the significance of the patterns in language and how challenging one of these patterns can bring about a major change in someone's experience and success.

A couple of months later, Grant sent me this feedback:

'I now have a picture of a woodland coppice with a carpet of bluebells stretching out in all directions to the near horizon. The deep blue and purple is so vivid that it is not difficult to imagine being there with my wife and daughter walking through the wood enjoying the perfume of the flowers and the gentle noises of nature getting on with its business.

Sitting here at my desk looking at that picture prompted me to do some more reflection on my outcome thinking. I felt that although I had identified an outcome I hadn't thoroughly identified what would make it happen so I have put together on paper a vision of me of who I am, what I do, and why I do it that will ultimately result in the "bluebell wood". In addition to that I have put on paper what actions I have to take in order to become that person. These actions are within my influence so it is up to me to pursue them and not to rely on the 6 numbers on a lottery ticket!

I have found that through my outcome thinking and conscious efforts my language is more positive and I am gradually eliminating the self-defeating elements and often find myself correcting the language I use in conversation. As I do more of this I believe I will use this outcome oriented language more naturally and therefore achieve greater success in achieving what I want.

The key messages for me really revolve around the value of observing behaviour and language and bringing this awareness into the conscious mind. This was totally reflected in my experience on the programme that you ran and I think this is the key to it all really – making the unconscious conscious and releasing the power that the mind holds. It is also very clear to me about the importance of helping the person being coached to realise that they do have all the resources that they need to bring about change and create a new reality! By making people aware of what they do now and what they want to do in the future you give that person choice. As you say in your first book "people make the best decision available to them at the time that they make it" and by raising awareness I believe the quality of those decisions improve.'

During the Napoleonic wars a lieutenant and his platoon were retreating from the enemy forces that had reached the periphery of the village where the platoon had taken temporary shelter. They suddenly heard sounds that made them realize that they were closer to the enemy than they had thought. There were too many of the enemy for them to attempt to defend themselves and so they looked for places to hide.

When the lieutenant was sure that his men had all found hiding places, he searched for one for himself. In desperation, he ran into a nearby house and begged the owner to hide him. The owner pointed to a pile of furskins on the floor and told him to get beneath them. The lieutenant did so and the owner covered him up. At that very moment, some of the enemy troops burst into the house and started to search everywhere. Eventually they saw the furs and thrust their bayonets into the pile. Not finding anything, they took a final look around and left.

When the owner was sure that the enemy had left, he told the lieutenant he was safe to come out and that the enemy troops had moved on out of the village. The lieutenant crawled out from under the furs, shaken but not injured. The owner of the house was amazed and asked the lieutenant how he had felt when he heard the soldiers thrusting their bayonets at him. The lieutenant grabbed the owner by the arms and marched him out of his home. He called his troops out of hiding and lined them up as a firing squad. He stood the owner in the firing line of the troops and ordered the troops to prepare to fire. The owner of the house shook all over and fell to his knees. The lieutenant walked over to him and lifted him from the floor. 'Now you have the answer,' he said.

This story offends and intrigues me. It stays with me in my thinking from when I first heard it several years ago. And it reminds me over and over again how to give the answer.

THOUGHT PROVOKERS

High-performance coaching is based on modeling your own or others' structure, i.e. discovering the conscious and unconscious structure for how we do what we do. The underlying question to get to this structure is: 'How do you do that?' (as opposed to why).

1   Identify an issue or a result in your life in which you would like more choices and understanding. Whatever it is that you do, ask yourself: 'How do I do that?' This question presupposes that there is something you do that gets you the results you get. What are the patterns that are yours? Even if you don't get an answer to your question immediately, be patient – the answer sometimes comes in the form of an experience rather than a piece of knowledge. There is nothing the unconscious likes better than a question and it will find an answer for you one way and one time or another. The skill lies in asking the right questions and being open to the answers.

2   If someone comes to you for coaching, first of all be sure that they are asking you to coach them. NLP is primarily a tool to be used for you and only with permission with others. Keep your questions to 'how' questions and similar. Examples of these are: 'How are you doing that?' 'How is that happening?' 'What is important to you about that?' 'What would you really like to have happen instead of that?' 'What would you like from me?' Check how you are in rapport with them and listen with your whole body. That in itself can influence insight and change. Give objective behavioral feedback, e.g. 'Did you know that when you say that you do this?' Keep feedback free of judgments about meaning.

3   Write down the thoughts you had in response to question 1. Look for any patterns in your language. If you read Grant's feedback on his one-to-one session, for example, you may notice which senses he uses predominantly in his comments. Do the same with your own writing.

Telemarketing and Call Centers   16

I keep the telephone of my mind open to peace, harmony, health, love and abundance. Then whenever doubt, anxiety, or fear try to call me, they keep getting a busy signal and soon they'll forget my number.

Edith Armstrong

WHEN I am traveling around I often rely on the directory enquiries service provided by mobile phone operator Cellnet to find the numbers I need. I particularly like the fact that the operator can dial the number on my behalf, saving me the hassle of struggling to key in the code when I am laden down with briefcase and bags. It surprised me how often the operator spoke in an Irish accent. It never occurred to me until I mentioned this in conversation with someone that the call center for this directory enquiry service could be in Ireland!

Such is the development of the technology that we use today that those who provide us with a service can be in any part of the world. To communicate with one of my suppliers who is in the process of upgrading all her equipment and who has not yet sorted out her e-mail, I e-mail to her father several hundred miles away who then relays the messages when he makes his daily call to her. When I have had a problem with Internet mail, I have had my queries answered from the US. In so many ways we are closing the gaps between the parts of the world that were once limited by the vast oceans in between. Now computers and telephony bridge the landmass and span the oceans and the seas. These systems bring together people who in some cases and in other circumstances may be at war with each other.

It requires a special skill to manage this faceless method of communicating. If your fingers are not used to typing, then your dexterity or lack of it may affect your fluency. If your preferred method of communicating is through visual means, then the absence of face-to-face contact may restrict your thinking and your effectiveness.

An opportunity to excel

Conversely, this provides an opportunity to excel and to develop new leading-edge skills that will encourage customers and suppliers to choose you. Each new market has its gap, a gap that exists through lack of thought or lack of skill. The awareness of what is needed is high. As in sport, the difference that makes the difference is the discipline to manage the finer points, to learn continuously and to improve and find the unique selling point in the way you do business.

On a recent occasion when I called directory enquiries to get the number of my car-servicing center, I asked for the name of the company and explained that it was a garage. I didn't say what type of garage it was. She found the number and read the description: Jaguar service center. 'Oh lucky you, I wish I had a Jaguar!' she added. I was very amused by this personal contact – the comment transformed the nature of the call.

Of course, this was a risk – some people might be offended by a personal comment. The skill lies in knowing what style to use with which person. Far from being impersonal, a telephone call can be very involving and can influence the way you perceive the quality of the service you are receiving from this supplier.

My associate's father who is currently acting as

intermediary for my e-mails has a very fluent and humorous style of communicating. His e-mails leave me with a smile and an anticipation of the next contact. I will regret the time when we no longer need him as an intermediary and I am already asking myself how else we could use his skill in the business.

I would suggest that this is the effect you always want to have on your customers – leaving them wanting to find ways to deal with you because they enjoy and value the contact irrespective of the content of the communication. So just what is the difference that makes the difference in this new and emerging market? How can you develop skills that will enable you to excel? One company exploring exactly that question and developing the skill to excel is Save & Prosper.

Leave them wanting to work with you

SAVE & PROSPER

Save & Prosper is one of Britain's oldest financial services groups offering a wide range of financial products, including PEPs, unit trusts, pension plans and banking services. In recent years the company's contact with its customers has increasingly been by phone. The cost of face-to-face selling and the rising number of clients have meant that the former style of client meetings has become prohibitive.

Save & Prosper has begun to set up teams whose role it is to make contact by phone. An example is the Intermediary Direct team, which sells Save & Prosper services over the phone to brokers. Its members are responsible for managing accounts and promoting new products. The team was formed early in 1997 and as such is setting a precedent for some methods of working that may develop in the future in other areas of the business.

Some members of the team already had telephone sales experience, but most did not. What they did have was enthusiasm to learn and excellent rapport as a group. Each person was knowledgeable and keen to know how they could best support the brokers with whom they dealt.

They recognized that the brokers were more often than not pushed for time (if you have ever seen brokers at work you will know that theirs is a high-speed business), so they needed to know not only how to use the phone to influence but how to do this in the most time-efficient way.

Save & Prosper invested in this team, together with others in the company, to develop both their identity as a team and their skill in making sales over the phone. The team went through a two-module program introducing them to the skills of NLP. In particular, they learned how to influence, how to be sensitive and how to build rapport. These skills were as valid for how they worked with each other as they were for how they dealt with their customers. Save & Prosper was enlightened in offering training that would help their staff with other areas of their life as well as what happened in the hours when they were at work. The bigger message in the way the company provided training and in what was offered was that it cared about its people as people and not just as 'work hands'.

THE MEANING OF THE COMMUNICATION IS THE EFFECT

The Intermediary Direct team members attended the training together, which also gave them time with each other socially in the coffee breaks and at the end of the day's program. They often talked about their leisure interests and hobbies. One member of the team was talking about their ambition for the sport in which they took part. In doing so, she expressed her doubts that she could achieve those ambitions. What the rest of the group did on this and similar occasions demonstrated a typical reaction for people who want to influence the thinking of the other person but who don't make the most effective choice in doing so. They told this person what they would do if they were in the same position, i.e. what works for them. They did not immediately notice that she was not changing her state either physiologically or verbally, i.e. she was not buying what they were saying. In fact, as soon as she had a chance she responded with a defense of

what she felt in a sentence that started with 'Yes, but...'
Have you noticed how it is possible to know when the
response you are going to get to a suggestion you have
made is going to be 'Yes but....' long before the person
opens their mouth to say the words themselves?

'Yes, but...'

What the group learned to do was to develop their
sensitivity to the signals the other party was giving them.
Initially they did this by watching body language and
eventually they concentrated on the language and the way
the other person spoke. They became skilled at detecting
when there was a shift in state, which tended to be a
unique signal for each person with whom they dealt. They
listened for tone of voice, intonation, shifts in pace,
volume and pitch.

They recognized that if what they wanted was a shift in
opinion or an acceptance of what they were presenting,
this would be indicated with a parallel shift in voice and
vocabulary. They became aware that the meaning of their
communication, in other words the success of their
influence, would be indicated by the type of response that
they got. No matter what sales procedure they used, if it
wasn't working then they needed to do something else.
The only measure of whether the approach they were
using was working was the response. In summary:

- The meaning of the communication is the effect.
- If what you are doing isn't working then do something
  else, otherwise if you do what you always did you get
  what you always got.

So often these presuppositions are missing from more
traditional sales training that encourages salespeople to
use an approach without the crucial sensitivity and
flexibility. The fact that this team was working
predominantly over the phone was no exception to this.
Language and the way it is spoken contain all the clues
necessary to know how successful your communication is
being.

AN ALTERNATIVE TO TELLING

The team began to realize the importance of finding out the underlying needs of the clients with whom they dealt so that they could show how their products met these needs. They learned how to identify the criteria for each of their clients so they could explore how they could meet these criteria, instead of presenting solutions that only met their own criteria. This is such a temptation in selling – to present your products in a way that fits for you but not necessarily for the other person.

They learned to ask questions in a way that was in line with the goals they wanted to achieve. They needed to be skilled in finding out the needs of their clients and they needed to be able to ask questions in a way that permitted their clients to come to conclusions that totally fitted with who they were and what they wanted.

The ability to recognize language patterns and the skill of selecting questions to challenge those patterns were among the main early developments in the use of NLP. This skill is crucial to sales and influencing. Clients who are encouraged to explore for themselves how products and services meet their needs will come to conclusions to which they have a far higher level of commitment than if the solution is prescribed for them.

For example, if someone doesn't think they can achieve their goal, asking the question 'What would have to be true for you to believe that you could?' prompts them to think consciously about what they need. This is infinitely more valuable and effective than asking them 'Why not?', which invites your listener to uncover consciously the reasons for their belief that they *cannot* achieve. If you really want to entrench them into the position of 'can't do', then this is the way to do it! However, if you really want them to go beyond the obstacles in their thinking, asking them 'What would happen if you did achieve your goal even though I appreciate that you think you can't?' invites them to step beyond the obstacles into what is possible.

Most salespeople have goals, but not everyone translates those goals down to moment by moment in their conversation. The skill you have with the questions you use is a measure of your ability to do this.

There are examples below of the goals that you might have in your everyday work conversations and some of the questions you could ask to achieve them:

GOALS	
To enable your listener to know consciously what stops them achieving what they want, e.g. they say 'I know what I want but I am not sure I can achieve it'	What stops you?
To check your understanding of who someone is referring to when they refer to them in a non-specific way, e.g. they say 'My client has a problem'	Who exactly do you mean?
To be sure you know what someone means by an action that they have expressed in an abstract way, e.g. they say 'OK, I will follow this through'	How exactly can/did/could you do that?
To find out someone's criteria, e.g. they say 'You haven't explained how this fits in with the bigger picture' or 'I need to know what is happening in XYZ market'	What is important to you about that?

Occasionally the team would meet the clients with whom they dealt on the phone, but this was rare. When they did meet, however, they were often surprised about how the appearance of the client varied from the way they had

imagined they would look. In particular, they realized that the way they imagined the clients they liked, even though they couldn't see them, was colorful, bright, life size, sitting back smiling. In contrast to this, the way they imagined someone with whom they did not get on so well and with whom they were less successful was often dark and dim. They pictured them with their arms folded and a stern expression on their face. Often clients who were less liked appeared larger than life in the person's imagination. They realized that they had these images already formed in their mind long before they made the telephone call. In some cases, the individuals realized that this was part of the reason that they put off making calls to these clients.

Of course, after realizing this the team had an opportunity to build some new, more appealing pictures, with the result that they felt differently about these clients. They chose to make these pictures the same as the ones that they held for the clients they liked and with whom they got on well.

SOUNDS GOOD TO ME

The immediate impression you make on the phone is with your voice. The way you sound and what you say are more important in this kind of work than in many others. The goal is to build rapport as quickly and as deeply as possible.

You can have rapport before you even engage in conversation

I was amused when someone who had done an overview of this kind of training elsewhere said that they could now build rapport within 15 minutes on the phone where once it had taken them half an hour. I appreciate that this was a 50 percent improvement for them, but in this kind of work you don't have the luxury of 15 minutes. If you don't have immediate rapport then you have lost an opportunity. I believe it is possible to have rapport in your thinking and in your expectation well before you engage in the conversation. And when you do engage you can immediately deepen that rapport.

To do this, it is crucial that you are skilled in listening to what the person on the other end of the line tells you and more especially *how* they tell you. The more you can match their style of speaking, the more chance you have to deepen that rapport. I have said elsewhere in this book that people like people who are like themselves. In the case of telemarketing and people working in call centers, it is a case of people liking people who talk and sound like themselves.

You can listen for the following:

- What words does the person use?
- What is the distinctive sound of their voice?
- What is the volume?
- How fast or slow do they speak?
- What is the tone of their voice?
- What is the intonation?
- What pauses do they use and when?
- What resonance does their voice have?
- Which senses dominate in their language?
- What filters do they use?

If you can recognize each of these then you can learn how to match them. When you match you build rapport. Maybe you are one of those people who find themselves adopting the accent of the person to whom you are speaking without consciously thinking about it. Often people have asked me if they should try to stop doing that in case the other person feels they are making fun of them. I reply that provided they have respect and they care for the person with whom they are speaking, then they can treat it as a measure of the rapport they have and at the same time be sensitive to the reactions of the other person (which I suspect they are more than likely to be already).

One of the Intermediary Direct team members asked me how they could do this and have a conversation at the same time. If you drive, think about how you learned to drive. Did you go straight to the busiest road you could and try all the trickiest maneuvers at once? I suspect not. I learned to drive on quiet, relatively unused roads and I mastered one maneuver at a time. It is the same with any skill. Avoid practicing all that you have learned with your most challenging client – save something for later down the line. Start by listening to people speaking on the radio. Take one of the above elements at a time until you can recognize it automatically. Then gradually do the same in meetings of which you are a part but in which you don't have a major role to play; ones in which you are more of an observer. Then begin to practice matching one thing at a time and then maybe for only 10 minutes at a time. Match and pace your own methods of learning. Choose what works for you in a way that gives you repeated successes on which to build.

Bear in mind the stages of learning. We often do not know what we are not skilled at until that lack of skill is tested one day or someone gives us feedback. This is the level of **unconscious incompetence**. When you get the feedback or have the realization of what you are not doing, you are at the level of **conscious incompetence**. It is likely that out of habit you continue to do what you have always done, even though you know you know that it is not what you want to be doing. You are still at the level of conscious incompetence. It may not feel like it, but you are learning and this is an important stage in the learning process. Now you have a planned means of behaving and you have to consciously work at it. It takes time and thought and effort, but you do succeed and reach **conscious competence**. Do this for long enough (some say it takes nine months to learn a new skill fully) and you will make it part of your automatic choice and your natural style – **unconscious competence**.

Genie Laborde's book 90 *Days to Communication Excellence* directs you to pay attention to one new element of behavior every few days. This is simple, but it works.

Some years ago Neil ran a coffee bar in the heart of the city of Liverpool. He prided himself on his establishment's fashionable décor and the style of his clientele. The coffee bar was busy in the afternoons and evenings but there was often a quiet period about 4 p.m. One day Neil was cleaning the highly polished counter when someone he had not seen before entered the bar. This new customer looked very out of place. He was dressed in what could only be described as hiking clothes: a dark blue anorak, a hand-knitted sweater and a woolly hat. Neil looked disdainfully at the man and asked him what he wanted.

'A coffee, please,' the man replied.

Neil reluctantly made the coffee and put it on the counter. 'That'll be 30p.'

The man reached into his pocket and took out three 10p coins. He put one down on the counter in front of Neil and then walked to the extreme left-hand end of the counter, where he put down the second 10p piece. Then he walked to the extreme right-hand end of the counter and put down the third 10p.

Neil was fuming; he could feel his face and neck getting red with anger but he didn't say anything. He walked down the full length of the counter and picked up the money. The man drank his coffee and left.

The following day, at the same time the same thing happened. Neil recounted the incidents to his friends, his regular clientele when they arrived that evening. He told them that somehow he was going to get his own back on this man if he came in again. He invited his friends to come earlier the next day so that they could be witnesses to this sport.

Sure enough, the next day the man arrived on time in the same outfit and asked for a coffee. Neil put the coffee down as usual and asked for the 30p. The man reached into his pocket and took out a 50p piece and placed on the counter in front of him. Neil smiled gleefully – this was his chance. He winked at his mates who were wondering what he was going to do.

Neil went to the till and took out two 10p pieces for the change. With a wry smile on his face, he looked at the man and walked down to the extreme left of the counter and put down one of the 10p pieces. He then walked down to the extreme right of the counter and placed there the other 10p. He returned to the middle of the counter and looked at the man.

The man didn't flinch. He picked up his cup, drank the coffee down, reached into his pocket, took out another 10p piece, placed it in the middle of the counter in front of him and said: 'Another coffee, please!'

THOUGHT PROVOKERS

1   Think of someone with whom you have contact but whom you have never met. If you have two people who fit this category for you, then think about them both. If there isn't anyone you know but have never met, do you have some for whom this was the case in the past although you have met them now? If so, then use these people in your thinking now. Think first of someone you like less well or is the least preferred of those you have identified. How do you imagine them? List as many of the visual attributes as you can. Colorful or black and white? Dark or light? Hazy or distinct? How do you imaging them to be sitting or standing? Smiling or serious? What is their posture? Now do the same with the person you like best and with whom you have the easiest communication. What are the distinctions between the way you think about each?

2   Think of someone you expect to telephone within the next few days. What is your expectation of this call? Do you expect to achieve your outcome with them? Do you expect to be able to support them in achieving theirs? Do you expect to be in rapport with them or not? Do you expect the conversation to be an easy one or not?

3   What are you aware of that you do in conversation that you wish you didn't? What do you do in conversation that pleases you when you do it but that you have to concentrate on to ensure that you actually do it?

4   Think of someone with whom you have to interact to get your job done. What is important to this person – what are their criteria and how do you go about meeting these?

17 *Trainer Training*

The soul and mind and life are powers of living and can grow, but cannot be cut out or made … One can indeed help the being to grow … but even so, the growth must still come from within.

Sri Aurobindo, *The Life Divine*, 1949

GONE are the days of 'chalk and talk'. We are now in the days of skilled facilitation, powerful presentation and influence by example. Successful trainers are in a different league to the teachers of old. The question is, who trains the trainers and how?

The NLP training I attended was run by the UKTC (UK Training Centre) and the weekend and midweek practice sessions were held at London Business School in Regents Park, London. At that time I lived in Wokingham in Berkshire, so it was quite a trek to get to the training venue. All of this says a lot to me about the motivation that I had for a subject that at that time I didn't really understand and certainly couldn't explain to anyone!

I missed the first weekend of training as I had something already in my schedule that I couldn't change, so I joined the group on module 2. I thought I had joined some obscure cult when I walked through the door to the coffee room. One of the trainers gushed an American welcome at me. The participants looked a motley crew and I chose to make conversation (or rather, attempt to make) with the one person who as far as I can remember didn't pass the course. Looking back, there were clear signs in that first conversation as to why he might not! I began to fear for the hard-earned money I had invested in the course. The group had studied and practiced rapport building in the weekend I had missed and I remember feeling distinctly uncomfortable as I watched them match anything that moved. Elegant it was not!

I refer to that first evening in Chapter 12, The inner team, as this was when we were introduced to the NLP presuppositions. I remember one bold participant in the group of 50 (yes, 50!) argue with the meaning of these presuppositions. I quickly learned that to argue was to incur the total phychotherapeutic attention of the tutor team, either then or later. I learned to smile and keep quiet. I did not know then the depth of those presuppositions, as was the case with many of the other concepts I came across then. They have many skins and to peel off one is to reveal another deeper and more meaningful one beneath. I have not stopped peeling since...

On day 2 of this module the lead trainer arrived, Gene Early. What I thought of as a stereotypical American – tall, good-looking, white-toothed smile, with the trace of a Memphis drawl. At this point in my training career I had already set up in business on my own. I had a comprehensive portfolio of clients and I was earning quite a bit more than what I had estimated I needed to keep petrol in the car and food on the table. I was successful as a training consultant and yet here was someone whose style took me aback. From the very first moment I could see that Gene Early was in control. He had the attention of the whole group without exception (even the attention of my nonconversation partner of the previous evening who normally sat at the back reading comic strips). Gene Early was engaging in every sense of the word.

He had the attention of the whole group

I was fascinated and now it was on a number of counts – the content, this mystical and challenging NLP and now the way it was being presented. Here was a model of excellence and I determined somewhere within myself to model this style, even though I did not yet understand what modeling meant in the way that I was about to learn through NLP.

THE MEDIUM OF THE MESSAGE

I know of training schools that still use some of the same exercises that we experienced then, over 10 years ago; I have to admit to using the odd one or two myself. The exercises were good, but that is not the point of NLP. The point is to be modeling and discovering your own exercises and insights for yourself. A legitimate practitioner of NLP is someone who is working real time with what is happening within themselves and with what is happening in the world today; they model what it is to train from the heart.

I have referred elsewhere in this book to the trainer who preached rapport only to elbow his way to the front of the coffee queue. And then there was the person who presented their ideas on influence and argued with those in his audience who disagreed with him. And I have experienced an audience of 'NLP practitioners' hiss at someone who made a comment that was considered to be unecological. Ugly is as ugly does.

Ugly is as ugly does

All of the delegates on one training program had the ambition of holding a senior post within the company. On the first of these programs there was one female delegate. At that time there were no women in senior posts in the company. This woman wanted to become a senior project manager – a demanding role for anyone in the company, let alone someone who would be setting a precedent in this position.

To be a senior project manager required willingness and a skill to manage projects anywhere in the world. It involved leading teams not only of company employees but also of local contractors, many of whom could be aggressive in their ways of working and responding to management. Even so, it wasn't the future role that was bothering this delegate as much as her everyday dealings with one of her colleagues. This colleague consistently pointed out what was wrong with just about everything she did and he did so in a particularly unpleasant and (she felt) aggressive way. Whatever the truth of the situation, she believed that her colleague wanted to obstruct her promotion into a more senior post. As a result of this, she was feeling inhibited and preoccupied by the responses she was getting from him.

It was the sessions on presuppositions that brought the breakthrough for her, in particular the presupposition that 'behind every behavior there is an unconscious positive intention towards you'. This can be one of the most challenging presuppositions to get your head around, but it can be one of the most powerfully liberating ones too. The ability to act as if this presupposition were true leads to a process of continuous learning — one of the most significant outcomes for this training.

We challenged her to create an unconscious positive intention behind the behavior of this colleague towards her. She struggled with this for some time and then had a revelation. To deal with him she needed to be able to deal with his aggression and her belief that he was seeking to keep her from being promoted. She suddenly realized that she needed this very skill — the skill of being able to handle aggression — to be successful in her desired future role as a senior project manager. So she chose to believe that every time this colleague responded to her with aggression, he was giving her practice in handling aggression, which was of course one of the skills she most needed. If she could handle him, she would be learning to handle some of the onsite contractors that she would have to deal with in the future.

She rushed back to work to face this colleague that she had previously avoided, delighting in the knowledge that every time she dealt with him she was getting on-the-job training in the valuable skill of handling aggression. There was also a secret amusement in the knowledge because he did not know that rather than thwarting her development (as was her original belief about him) he was, on the contrary, contributing to her growth every time he made a sarcastic or cutting remark! And she did fulfill her ambitions.

WHAT DOESN'T MAKE A DIFFERENCE?

When I first joined what was then the English Electric Engineering training department, my manager sent me on the only Instructional Techniques course that he knew of and would recommend – the one that he had attended in the RAF! I was 21 years old, the only woman on the site and the only civilian. This was an experience I shall never forget. I owe a lot to that course. I learned to ask for help by ringing for the batman when I discovered that I couldn't get my new knee-high leather boots off. I learned not to stand up for something at the breakfast table unless I wanted all the officers present instantaneously to drop their cutlery and stand to attention. I learned from the presentations given by my fellow delegates on the course how to calculate the maximum take-off weight of a VC-10, how to evacuate a plane on crash landing and how to protect your ear drums when flying with a headcold (basically, don't fly!).

There is no doubt that I also learned essentials that stood me in very good stead for years: How to structure a training session. How talk for at least three minutes without looking at your notes. How to write those notes so you can imperceptibly glance at them when your mind has gone blank and detect the prompt from a distance of at least six feet that would keep you going for another five minutes. Another gem was how to walk as you write so that the lines of writing on the chalkboard didn't disappear into the bottom right-hand corner as you remained fixed to one spot on the floor.

I jest – I learned a lot and I am very grateful for all that I did learn there. It meant that I could generate enough courage when talking to a group so that I wanted to turn back from writing on the chalkboard and face them again. But I believe it was only when I participated in NLP courses that I began to learn what really made a difference. And then I was fascinated and mesmerized. I had the privilege of learning from trainers that I consider to be the best of the best in the world today.

I have already described Gene Early and for me he still

is the best. I also experienced Robert Dilts, one of the most innovative developers and modelers in NLP. David Gordon brought humor and reality to my star-struck state. I will never forget his introduction to us NLP fanatics, as I believe most of us were at that time: 'Anyone who lives, breathes and eats NLP is sick!' Barbara Witney was another trainer who joined us for a module. You may never have heard of these names, but if you ever do and if you want to experience some of the best trainers in the field, then I recommend you go and see them and model them.

DISCOVERIES AND RESULTS

There may be some of you who want gimmicks – the easy answer, the quick fix – and there are plenty of those in what has been discovered through NLP. There is impressive magic that you can learn and trot out as a party trick when you want to impress. But I would not be being honest with you if I said that these were really what makes the difference. I have modeled many trainers and continue to do so, and what I have discovered is not always an easy answer. Some of these discoveries require a major investment in time and energy. Nevertheless, I will share them with you and the choice is yours. It may be that you do these things already. It may be that you know differently. I would love to know: I am always open to discovering more of what really makes the difference.

There are plenty of quick fixes

So what are these discoveries? I would sum them up as commitment, practicing what you preach, connection, creating experiences from which to learn and not knowing the answers. Simple? The question is what exactly I mean by these statements and how exactly you do these things. This is also not to say that what I learned at RAF Upwood wasn't important – it was. It gave me a foundation from which to be open to these new ways of training.

I measure success by the results that the trainees who shared my initial training achieved. Many are now major contributors to the wealth of discoveries through NLP.

Many have diversified and developed their own specialization. For me it was NLP in business.

What are those results? The fact that many people do still use the exercises we used then, which is testimony to both the lasting power and the impact of those exercises. The fact that many people faced major crossroads in their lives and made decisions that have subsequently been experienced as a win–win for all affected by them. And more than anything else, the fact that the learning from that training continues. It was as if we were given something rather like those flu-relieving tablets that release themselves over time. We were given learning capsules that continue to fire off when the timing is right or when we need them most. This was at a time before concepts such as the learning organization had been developed, yet those trainers had equivalent concepts then. They were well ahead of their time in many ways; of course in many others they were absolutely right for their time and continue to be so.

They practice what they preach

The main reason that they were and still are at the top of their profession is that they practice what they preach. They are without exception people who are curious, who are constantly developing what they do and as a result they are continuously learning. I am often asked if I think NLP is a one-day wonder. The best way I can answer is to point to those people who have studied it and who continue to apply what they learn.

I would expect any trainer, whether they are training NLP or any other topic, to be skilled in their ability to do the following:

- build rapport with everyone they train and maintain it throughout all of their contact
- adapt their style so that they can present their thoughts and ideas in a way that fits with the thinking style of the person with whom they are dealing
- be sensitive to how people are responding to them both verbally and nonverbally
- be flexible in the choices they have for how they think

and how they behave

- manage their state so that they are always in a state that is supportive of the training they are doing
- use enriched language so that they appeal to all the styles of a mixed group
- design training programs that appeal to all of the senses so that people with all learning styles are catered for
- recognize patterns in language, both in themselves and in the people they are training, and challenge them when appropriate to do so
- put themselves in other people's shoes and stand back in order to create a situation of learning
- act out of the NLP presuppositions, especially ones such as:
  - there is no failure only feedback
  - people make the best choices available to them
  - people have all the resources within them to achieve what they want
  - the meaning of the communication is the effect
  - the map is not the territory
- set outcomes for themselves and their training in such a way that they consistently achieve them

And if that isn't enough, I will now explain what I have discovered to be the difference that really makes the difference!

YOU CANNOT KNOW ENOUGH

There is a paradox in being a good trainer – you need to know everything there is to know that you can study, discover and practice. You cannot know enough. There was once a time when I would have said that what you present should be the tip of the iceberg, but I realized that I held a different belief when I was asked by one of my delegates how much you should give away at the initial meetings and in the initial training. I realized that my belief is that you should give away as much as you can as soon as you can, provided that it is relevant. I believe that by emptying yourself of everything you know (I don't mean lecturing non-stop; I do mean answering any questions you are asked as fully and as honestly and as openly as you can) you create space within yourself to learn more. Do a regular springclean and you have space to arrange the furniture in the way you really want it and to put in something new. So you need to be learning constantly and therefore not to know all the answers – and to say so and to show it.

The power of this for me is highlighted in the story at the end of the chapter. This is a part of what it means to live out the presupposition that there is no failure, only feedback. Everything that happens can be a source of learning if you believe this; the journey really is as good as the destination, or dare I say even better.

One of my colleagues challenged me regarding my role in the training that we were doing. 'What does it mean to sit at the front of the room, Sue?' she asked. 'Does it mean that you have less to learn than anyone else?'

We seek to position ourselves as co-learners. Experts aren't learners in my book. To be an expert presupposes right and wrong and often excludes learning. This may be controversial, but I believe it is true.

My experience is that those trainers who are modelers have an attitude of curiosity and they seek to understand how they and others are feeling, what they are feeling and how they are getting the results they are getting. The most aligned trainers are those who use their own experience to form the basis of what they offer to their course participants. If you start where you are, you can take a group with whom you have rapport to the goal by leading them there in your own experience.

We train by the example of who we are and not what we say. You always stand for something in what you do and the way you do it – the question is what you stand for.

Most teaching (if that is what we call it) is done to the unconscious mind. The skill for a trainer lies in knowing just what they are communicating to others' unconscious minds. You will have taught what you mean about rapport well before you talk about it. Will your words match your actions? What are you teaching to others' unconscious minds as you talk to their conscious mind? It isn't a choice as to whether to do this or not – you do it anyway – but it is a choice as to whether you do it skillfully or not.

Imagine that you are booking on to a course on influence and interpersonal skills. You contact the training company to make the booking and the person on the other end of the phone takes great care in finding out how they can help you. You feel that they understand your specific needs. You have questions about the training, some of which they answer and if they can't they arrange for someone to get back to you with the necessary information. You confirm your booking and you receive a personalized letter welcoming you as a participant in the training. All the questions you have about the arrangements are covered in this letter and you feel more and more comfortable about attending the course.

The day of the course arrives and you turn up at the venue. From the moment you get there you feel welcomed and already a part of the group. The tutors introduce themselves to you and show you around. You feel connected to them immediately and anticipate how much you are going to enjoy and learn from your time with them. This is pleasurable and you can begin to see how your needs will be met. You have a sense from what is said that you can explain any of your needs and they will be heard and addressed; and at the same time you sense that you will be challenged. In all of the sessions you experience a connection with not only the tutors but the other delegates in the way that the day and the exercises and introductions are organized. Later on that first day the tutors introduce the topic of rapport. Your unconscious mind has already experienced it.

Your unconscious mind has already experienced it

This is what it means to teach to the unconscious mind. This is what it means to be an example of what you present. This is whole-body learning.

WIN–WIN CONNECTIONS

When I attended the UKTC training programs I experienced attention that I wasn't used to. I eventually got the courage to express my thoughts and my needs, with the result that I received personal coaching and facilitation of a quality that I had not experienced before in the company of a larger group like this. What also surprised me was how the whole group was able to learn from the dedicated attention given to one person. The tutors (and they all did this without exception) stayed with the individual until they had resolved the issue. They committed themselves to support that person in the achievement of their outcomes. For some of the tutors this commitment lasted for that module, for some for the whole course and for some I believe that commitment had no end. Gene Early still works with me today in helping me to achieve my outcomes and in doing so he is achieving outcomes for himself. It is a total win–win.

A win–win

There are undoubtedly techniques that make this kind of **connection** possible. For example:

- the skill to monitor the whole group and to anchor learning for them while working predominantly with one person
- the ability to pay attention to process and content simultaneously
- the willingness to identify with the other so that you believe that whatever you recognize in them is true for you too; this is not something you are doing *to* them
- the ability to choose to show the answer in the way you respond as much if not more than in what you say
- the ability to know at what level the issue or the questioner presents itself and the skill to come back at a higher level

As Einstein is reported to have said: 'You don't solve a problem with the thinking that generated the problem in the first place.'

But I would say that more than anything else that what enables connection is having a purpose, which is to be there for others to support their learning. It is to be there as a friend if that other person chooses to respond to you in this way. The best trainers and consultants I know respect that if they are to introduce new concepts and ways of thinking to their participants, they have the responsibility to be there as a support for them if necessary.

If you have read this book, you have my commitment to you that if you need support or advice based on what I present here, then within my capability or the capability of my company acting on my behalf you will have it. You have only to ask.

The aim is to be there to support learning

At the age of fifteen, in the middle of my junior year, I quit Exeter, one of the most highly regarded preparatory schools in the nation. As I look back on that turning point in my life, I am amazed at the grace that gave me the courage to do it. Not only was I dropping out of a prestigious prep school against my parents' wishes, but I was walking away from a golden WASP track that had all been laid out for me. Hardly aware that it was what I was doing, I was taking my first giant step out of my entire culture. That culture of 'the establishment' was what one was supposed to aspire to, and I was throwing it away. And where was I to go? I was forging into the total unknown. I was so terrified I thought I should seek the advice of some of Exeter's faculty before finalizing such a dreadful decision. But which of the faculty?

The first candidate who came to mind was my advisor. He had barely spoken to me for two and a half years, but he was reputedly kindly. A second obvious candidate was the crusty old dean of the school, known to be beloved to tens of thousands of alumni. But I thought that three was a good round number, and the third choice was more difficult. I finally hit upon Mr Lynch, my Maths teacher, a somewhat younger man. I chose him not because we had any relationship or because he seemed to be a particularly warm sort of person – indeed, I found him a rather cold, mathematical kind of fish – but because he had a reputation for being the faculty genius. He's been involved with some kind of high-level mathematics with the Manhattan Project, and I thought I should check out what I was considering with a 'genius.'

I went first to my kindly advisor. He let me talk for about two minutes and then gently broke in. 'It's true that you're under-achieving here at Exeter, Scotty, but not so seriously that you won't be able to graduate. It would be preferable for you to graduate from a superior school like Exeter with lesser grades than from a lesser school with better grades. It would also look bad on your record for you to switch horses in midstream, Besides, I'm sure your parents would be quite upset, so why don't you just go along and do the best you can?'

Next I went to the crusty old dean. He let me speak for thirty seconds. 'Exeter is the best school in the world,' he harrumphed. 'Damn fool thing that you're thinking of doing. Now you just pull yourself up by the bootstraps, young man!'

Feeling worse and worse, I went to see Mr Lynch. He let me talk *myself out. It took about five minutes. Then he said he didn't yet understand, and asked if I would just talk some more about Exeter, about my family, about God (he actually gave me permission to talk about God!) – about anything that came into my head. So I rambled on for another ten minutes in all, which was pretty good for a depressed, inarticulate, fifteen-year-old. When I was done, he inquired whether I would mind if he asked me some questions. Thriving on this adult attention, I replied, 'Of course not,' and he queried me about many different things for the next half-hour.*

Finally, after forty-five minutes in all, this supposedly cold fish sat back in his chair with a pained expression on his face and said, 'I'm sorry. I can't help you. I don't have any advice to give you. You know,' he continued, 'it's impossible for one person to ever completely put himself in another person's shoes. But insofar as I can put myself in your shoes – and I'm glad I'm not there – I don't know what I would do if I were you, So, you see, I don't know how to advise you. I'm sorry that I've been unable to help.'

It is just possible that that man saved my life, and that I'm able to be sitting here writing this today because of Mr Lynch. For when I entered his office that morning over forty years ago, I was close to suicidal, and when I left I felt as if a thousand pounds had been taken off my back. Because if a 'genius' didn't know what to do, then it was all right for me not to know what to do. And if I was considering a move that seemed so insane in the world's terms and a genius couldn't tell me that it was clearly, obviously demented, well then maybe, just maybe, it was something God was calling me to.

So it was that man, who didn't have any answers or quick formulas, who didn't know what I should do and was willing to be empty, who was the one who provided the help I needed. It was that man who listened to me, who gave me his time, who tried to put himself in my shoes, who extended himself and sacrificed himself for me, who loved me. And it was that man who healed me. It was an extraordinary act of civility.

M Scott Peck

THOUGHT PROVOKERS

1 Who was the best teacher you had at school? What
   qualities did this person have that others did not?
2 Identify an incident with this teacher that you know will
   stay with you forever. What is it about this incident that
   makes it so memorable?
3 What learning did you gain from this person and how
   have you used that learning in your life?

Leadership 18

Lao-Tzu

*E*VER since Tom Peters highlighted the difference between management and leadership in his book *A Passion for Excellence*, there has been a reverence about the term leadership. I subscribe to the view that the future will be governed by teams of leaders. Consequently, we need to know how to recognize and enhance the exclusive qualities that are the lifeblood of a leader. I have often been asked: 'Are leaders born or can they be developed?' My view is that leadership qualities can be a mixture of both inherent traits as well as learned and developed ones.

The future will be governed by teams of leaders

FUJITSU COMPUTERS

NLP has a reputation for being a fast, powerful fix for personal and business issues that with other approaches might take three, four or sometimes many more times longer to resolve. And at the same time NLP is a way to manage the process of growth and development. An excellent example of this is Mike Campbell, vice-president – Europe for personnel at Fujitsu Computers, one of the fastest-growing PC businesses. He has grown himself and his contribution to the business over the years. Mike is by no means a traditional HR person, since he has a considerable input to business strategy. The challenge for Fujitsu is to find a job title that truly reflects what he does. This is in itself is a measure of success, showing that key people are no longer fulfilling traditional and familiar roles.

People no longer fulfill traditional roles

Mike has all the qualities of a leader and he will be the first to admit that he has not always had all of these; some have been developed and some have been learned. If there is one quality above all that has made this possible, it is his ability and passionate desire to learn. He has been open to new ways of thinking throughout his career and he has learned specific NLP techniques to manage his growth along the way. Mike is also – in his words – 'humble' and would probably rather that I had highlighted what he calls his 'warts', of which he says he is only too well aware.

Having worked with Mike on his development and having modeled what truly makes a difference for him in his industry, we have a profile of what has worked for him in growing his leadership skills. Above all, he demonstrates an awareness of what he does do that makes a difference and what he needs to develop. And this is constantly changing. He would be the first to admit that the skills he has today need constant review and updating. He has the awareness of what he does and its impact that is characteristic of a skilled modeler, although he would not use those words to describe himself.

What are his skills?

Setting compelling outcomes

He has the ability to set compelling outcomes for himself and the business and to achieve them consistently at the time he predicts. He has a vision for the business with clear indicators of success and has six-monthly staging posts. All the goals that he set for the business for the last three years have been achieved.

Probably what is most significant is that he worked with an international team to do this and so has been able to blend together the thinking and desires and very different cultural preferences in the process. In his own words:

'I *have the ability to accommodate a lot of variation to my initial vision which allows others to own it too.*'

This skill of working with others from different cultural backgrounds has grown from Mike's willingness to learn how others think and, even more significantly, his ability to accept the different ways in which others think and work. He has learned how to recognize the patterns in his own and others' language and behavior in such a way that he can see the uniqueness of each person's style. He has the flexibility not to place any judgment on those styles but to accept them for what they are. At the same time, he can match style to business requirements, both present and future, and can identify the implications of each style for the outcomes of the business.

Ability to work with people from different cultures

Mike would identify his ability to build rapport very definitely as a learned skill and one that has been an outstanding success. When challenged as to whether he might always have had this skill, his response is a totally congruent 'No'. He recognizes this ability to build rapport as priceless, given his need to work with members of the management team in Japan, Germany, Finland and the UK.

Learned rapport

Probably one of Mike's outstanding strengths is his ability to analyze a situation from an objective standpoint – another learned skill. And he is precise in his ability to model this in himself; he knows exactly how he does it:

Objective analysis

'I *have learned how to dissociate myself at two levels; I can stand back and see myself watching myself.*'

This skill of dissociation is characteristic of leaders and learners – it allows the person doing the standing back to see connections in the system as a whole. They can see themselves (as if from afar) in the bigger system. It is also

The ability to dissociate

characteristic of people who have the capacity to think systemically. This is a skill that we find in people who can deal rationally with traumatic events, people who can give and receive constructive feedback and those who are consistently successful in negotiating win–win outcomes. Being able to stand back in this way and see yourself as an observer means being able to dissociate from the emotions of the situation. In Mike's case, having this skill means that he can objectively see the holistic impact of someone on the company system as a whole.

Making connections

It is this ability to stand back and see the bigger picture that also contributes to Mike's ability to make connections between seemingly unconnected factors and circumstances. This is characteristic of people who have the capacity to think creatively and to devise innovative solutions to problems.

'*I am overwhelmed by the connections between mathematics and quantum mechanics and outcome thinking in NLP. Put simply – you can have an infinite number of outcomes and you determine an outcome by measuring it. To achieve the outcome you must be a part of it – you cannot sit outside of it to do so.*'

Reframing

Mike has the skill of reframing. He can choose the meaning that he makes of a situation in a way that works for him:

'*Where others see conflict I see benefit.*'

Mike would say that he has learned how to trust his intuition and if you have been modeling what I have reported of Mike you may have detected that another preferred sense is visual; he often uses visually descriptive words – vision, see, watching, the bigger picture. With this preferred sense he has a strong sense of feeling:

'*I can sense the energy in what I say.*'

MIKE'S BELIEFS AND VALUES

Behind these skills, both innate and learned, is a powerful set of presuppositions. Mike's experience of the presupposition 'there is a solution to every problem' (and it is more than a presupposition, it is a belief in his ability) is: 'I've got a crazy faith in my ability to solve any problem.' In respect of other people Mike says:

'I fully accept that people do things in the way that they can at the time that they do it. That is just the way that they are. There was a time recently when I would have really liked support from someone with whom I have often sought advice but they weren't there for me at that time and I accept that therefore they were not ready to help me then. I also accept that when they are ready they will make contact.'

He has a strong set of values, which underpin everything he does:

- Commitment: If I say I will do something for you then I will do it.
- Acceptance: I accept that we each think and act differently and that is what makes us unique. I can accept that and I know what is right for the business and what is not.
- Professionalism: is all about understanding expectations and working with people to meet those expectations; always seeking to do the best I can; anything less than my best is not good enough.
- Trust: is about working with people, with an implied commitment in that working relationship. I give people the freedom to do their job on trust. However, if that confidence or bond is broken, then it breeds suspicion in all areas of the relationship. I have learned that I can work with anyone but if I don't have the trust or it is broken the relationship doesn't progress.
- Customer focus: for me is about understanding and anticipating what the customer wants. It is also about the individuals in a team knowing their role and understanding how what they do contributes to the whole.
- Profitability: is a measure of success that is about sustainable profitability for now and the future. It's about building success for tomorrow.

Evidence of Mike's living out his values was reinforced by the reactions of some applicants for senior management posts who went through the interviewing process. These candidates were impressed by the very strong sense of image that came across from Mike and others on the selection team. These candidates sensed an alignment between the values that were stated and the way that those values were being lived out in practice.

In summary, what Mike identifies himself as having learned as a result of his training and consultancy with NLP are some of the techniques he uses, for example, to achieve his objectivity and the ability to have confidence in what he can do. He has consciously learned how to build rapport and to watch and listen to others in ways that he never would have done a few years ago. He has also learned how to congratulate himself and in so doing he is able to share those congratulations with the successes of his own team:

'What we give to others stems from what we are able to give ourselves.'

And overall Mike has a purpose:

'I want to make a difference and I want us to be a really good global company.'

And I have every confidence that if he has anything at all to do with this, it will.

YELLOW SUBMARINE

Personal and business congruence

If there is one thing that is common to all outstanding leaders, it is personal and business congruence. They are the example of what they stand for in everything they do.

The Yellow Submarine describes itself as a marketing exploration company. They are leaders in their field and are in a class of their own in their style in a business sector that is renowned for its aggressive manner. The Yellow Submarine claims values such as cooperation and growth; nothing unusual in that, you may say. The difference is that the team – or should I say crew – live them out in everything they do. It is one of the most aligned companies that I have encountered.

The company's environment is in the form of a yellow submarine with stainless steel fittings, portholes and a poop deck (I will leave it to you to work our which room that is!). A submarine does not have different levels and nor does this company, where the managers sit alongside the crew in open-plan offices. They seek to bring the creativity that constitutes their design excellence into the way they think about their business and the promotion of how they work. At a marketing design awards dinner, all the tables were identical (surprising, you may think, for an industry that is meant to be skilled in branding individual identity). Every table was laid out with white napkins, red flowers, and a white card with a black table number on a silver stand. Ten minutes before the dining room was opened to guests from many different companies, several Yellow Submarine staff found a way in to gain access to the two tables that were allocated to them and transformed them with yellow name markers, yellow flowers and large Yellow Submarine table markers. If your business is to promote the identity of a business in a memorable way, then you start with yourself.

The alignment in their environment is borne out in their management style and the effect of that on everyone who works there. The managers are some of the closest to what I would describe as servant leaders than in any other company I know:

Servant leaders

'*At a social event, it would not matter how you laid out the name place cards – I would be delighted to sit next to anyone in this company that I was placed next to.*'

One of the account directors (and this comment would be true for anyone in the business)

'This is the happiest I have ever been in my career.'
(I have not yet found anyone who works for this company who does not say this!)

Everyone is personally accountable

There is a price to pay for these exceptional working conditions – every member of the company is personally accountable to their client for the results. They don't have teams of minions to do the hard graft for them – they do it themselves. This can be a shock to anyone who is used to working in the more traditional form of marketing agency where there are teams of people to do the legwork. At the Yellow Submarine they 'walk the talk'.

CPL

Cegelec Projects Ltd (CPL) was once part of GEC but is now part of a large French organization. When it became French owned the need was to form a new culture – one with a new style of leadership that would enable the company to create new markets and new ways of working. The old culture had been problem centered and past facing and the management team decided it was time to take a longer-term view of the business and invest in the future. They recognized that if any of the existing management team were to retire, there was no one within the company ready to succeed them. They also recognized that there was a need to develop leaders for the future who would not just step into the shoes of the existing management team, but who would establish a new forward-looking culture in which there was greater ownership of the business as a whole.

The management team agreed a set of criteria that they believed would be characteristic of these potential high fliers. One of the most important criteria was that they were open to learning and growth; they did not currently need to have all the skills of a leader, but they needed to be willing to develop those that they did not currently possess.

Managers were invited to nominate suitable candidates. These initial nominees were then interviewed and a delegate team was selected. This team was the first of several who were put through the same process, setting a precedent for those who followed. A measure of success was that these candidates would be promoted on their merits and would be successful in their management of large projects for the company. This has proved to be the case.

The training included the skills of being able to:

- set compelling outcomes and communicate them in ways that were enticing to others in their teams
- build rapport with customers, colleagues, management and members of the teams they currently managed
- recognize unique ways of thinking and communicating
- define their unique contribution to the business and the measurement of their success in their skill in doing this

But most important of all were the skills of being able to:

- be in rapport with themselves, i.e. congruent and passionate in what they did and said
- learn continuously from every situation – seemingly good or bad
- take ownership of their own experience and their own development

More than anything, these young potential leaders learned how to challenge the patterns in their thinking and behavior. They especially learned how to recognize when they attributed blame to anyone outside of themselves and to take ownership of their contribution to the system. In other words, they learned that their experience was either as a result of their compliance with the bigger system of which they were a part, or it was as a result of their conscious choice to influence their environment, and they could choose which they wanted it to be.

THERE IS LEARNING IN EVERYTHING

THE RESULTS

Four years on from that initial training program, most of those delegates have become key players in the business. They mostly hold senior project management roles and have influenced many of the more senior managers. Some have acted as mentors to the existing managing director and members of the senior management team. It has now become an integral part of the program for them to act in this capacity.

The first group to do this training decided to promote the value of teamwork throughout the business. They promoted the value, they educated people in the company about what it meant and why it was important, and they introduced prizes and measures for teams who met the criteria. As you walk through the doors to the Cegelec offices in Rugby, you step on to a large mat that says 'Welcome to our team' – and they mean it. They did the training as a group alongside fulfilling their daily engineering work.

WELCOME
TO OUR
TEAM

Delegates who have been through this process (even one of those who left to have a family) are involved in subsequent programs, to advise, to coach and to act as mentors.

And the business? Cegelec has new markets and a growing reputation for success. A recent project for a leading metals manufacturer was completed ahead of schedule, exceeded all the customer's criteria and surpassed both the customer's and CPL's profit targets. The engineers involved in this project attribute its success predominantly to the quality of the teamwork, and they intend to ensure that what they have learned in the process will be shared and learned by other divisions in the business. Today, Cegelec truly has a culture of leadership and learning.

THE ACADEMY FOR CHIEF EXECUTIVES

Leaders learning with leaders

Leaders learning with leaders – who better to act as a friend, a support and a challenge than another leader? This is the principle behind this growing organization that expresses its values as goals:

- to care
- to share
- to be open
- to confront
- to act with integrity

Needless to say, leaders can be in the company of other leaders and still not learn. Doing so requires an ability to seek and receive feedback. This is one of the two most significant skills that the Academy supports in its members. The other is the ability of a leader to passionately live and express their goals for their business. Surprisingly, it is success that seems to be the greatest diluter of passion. As businesses succeed and grow there is a need for systems and procedures and the entrepreneurial flair and diversity that were the lifeblood of the new and growing business can, if not harnessed, be its very destruction.

Through its structure of monthly meetings with visiting speakers and through its one-to-one coaching sessions, the Academy seeks constantly to challenge its members to learn and grow. At the heart of this growth is the need sometimes to revitalize the emotions of leaders who have lost some of their original passion and energy. Each year the Academy organizes an event designed to do just that.

One of the processes that have made the difference in rekindling the entrepreneurial flame is the alignment of each leader's goals with the logical levels model. The result of this is either that the person's goals develop so that they are aligned at all levels or they change their goals.

These leaders combine this with developing their ability to put themselves into other people's shoes and the skills of giving and receiving feedback. This is a simple formula, but one that has powerful and sometimes astonishing results. One of the business leaders admitted that the first change he needed to make was with his mother. Only when he had shown her how much he loved her (which he admitted he had not really expressed in ways that she would recognize) would he be fit to lead his business.

A failing samurai warrior, fearing that he might die soon, went to see a wise old sage to face up to what might happen after death.

'I would like to know the difference between heaven and hell,' he asked the sage.

'You have spent your life fighting – you are too stupid to understand the difference between the two,' the sage replied.

The warrior was incensed. He flew into a rage and grabbed hold of the old man, thrusting his sword to the old man's throat. He was a hair's breadth from slitting the man's throat when he pulled back. The sage was unmoved.

'That is hell,' he said to the warrior.

The warrior was astonished. 'You risked your life to show me hell – you were within seconds of losing your life and you didn't flinch!'

'And that is heaven,' the wise old sage responded.

THOUGHT PROVOKERS

1   In what ways are you a leader both at home and at
    work?
2   What influence do you have on those around you? How
    does the influence you think you have compare with the
    influence you really have? Do you know? How could
    you find out?
3   What sort of a difference do you personally want to
    make in the world today?
4   What is your personal vision of the future?
5   How could you turn something that you consider to be
    currently hindering your personal growth into something
    that positively enhances it?

Appendix
Eye Accessing Cues

A clue to the way you think is given in the way you move your eyes. The usual way in which these eye movements are organized is as follows:

up and right (their right)
for constructed, imagined images
e.g. you floating on air or you with blue hair (assuming you haven't got or had blue hair!)

up and left
for remembered images
e.g. the scenes on your holidays, the image of your school

sideways right
for constructed sounds
e.g. your boss talking to you in a Donald Duck voice, the sound of a cat barking

sideways left
for remembered sounds
e.g. your favourite piece of music, the sound of a bath
running

down and right
for feelings and internal emotions
e.g. the touch of silk, the feeling of confidence or sadness

down and left
for internal dialogue
e.g. what you say to yourself before you give an important
presentation, or before you go to sleep at night

straight ahead, defocused
for visual images, remembered or created
e.g. the faces of your close friends, the way you imagine
the route might look on a journey you are about to take

These are the usual eye movements for right-handed
people, but there are exceptions. Left-handed people
may have some of the positions reversed.

Bibliography

I wondered what books to include in this bibliography, as so many have influenced my thinking over the years. I am a book addict. I cannot go through an airport without buying at least two or three books. I plan to travel light and I load myself down with books to read on the flight or at my destination, even though I will probably have packed three or four already. Books have been my reference, my guide and my inspiration. Some authors have such an elegant style that to read them is to be inspired to write and in particular to determine to write with elegance and fluency and compassion.

I have referenced other books of mine and those books that I had open at my side at some point during my writing. Some are mentioned in the text; some were there in my background thinking at most times. If there are ones here that you have not yet read, then I wish you the pleasure and inspiration in reading them that they gave me.

NLP *at Work*, Sue Knight, Nicholas Brealey Publishing, 1995.

Personal Selling Skills, Sue Knight, Sue Knight Books & Talks.

MORE BOOKS ON NLP

NLP: *the New Technology of Achievement*, Steve Andreas &
    Charles Faulkner, Nicholas Brealey Publishing, 1996.
Strategies of Genius, Robert Dilts, Meta Publications, 1996.
Influencing with Integrity, Genie Z Laborde, Syntony, 1983.
Introducing Neuro-linguistic Programming, Joseph O'Connor and
    John Seymour, Thorsons, 1993.
Training with NLP, Joseph O'Connor and John Seymour,
    Thorsons, 1994.
Living Awareness, Peter Wrycza, Gateway Books, 1997.

BACKGROUND READING

The Seven Habits of Highly Effective People, Stephen R. Covey,
    Simon & Schuster, 1992.
Waiting for the Mountain to Move, Charles Handy, Arrow, 1995.
The Hungry Spirit, Charles Handy, Arrow, 1998.
Synchronicity, Joseph Jaworski & Betty S Flowers, Berrett
    Koehler, 1998.
A World Waiting to Be Born, M Scott Peck, Rider, 1993.
A Passion for Excellence, Tom Peters & Nancy Austin,
    HarperCollins, 1986.
Real Cooking, Nigel Slater, Michael Joseph, 1997.
The Fifth Discipline, Peter Senge, Century/Arrow, 1993.
The Fifth Discipline Fieldbook, Peter Senge *et al.*, Nicholas
    Brealey Publishing, 1994.

Glossary

Anchoring The process of making associations that work through conscious choice so that you can reaccess your own or trigger others' chosen state when appropriate.

Association The state of being inside your own skin, seeing the world from your own eyes, hearing the world from your own ears and feeling the emotions of the situation, whether current, remembered or imagined.

Beliefs Emotionally held opinions treated as facts and the basis of our everyday decisions, skills and behaviors.

Congruence Having all parts of yourself working in harmony; being at one with yourself.

Criteria The values and standards used as the basis for decisions.

Dissociation The state of observing yourself as if you were an outsider. Seeing and hearing yourself from the outside, i.e. you can see you in your entirety not the way you see yourself from within your own body. The effect of dissociation is to disconnect from emotions.

Eye accessing cues Movements of a person's eyes that indicate visual, auditory or kinaesthetic (feelings) thinking.

Filters Levels of thinking that determine where we put our attention and consequently what constitutes perception. These filters determine how we respond to situations and people.

Linguistic The study of language and in the context of NLP the patterns in language that communicate our thinking strategies.

Logical levels A form of personal and organizational hierarchy that impacts on change and how effectively we bring about change for ourselves or for others. Consisting of environment, behavior, capabilities, values, beliefs, identity and purpose.

Metaphor Having a parallel means of describing or observing. Metaphors can be parables, stories, analogies, pictures, actions. Often used to influence the unconscious mind and bypass conscious resistance.

Modeling The process of unpacking our own and others' conscious but especially unconscious strategies in order to duplicate the results achieved.

Neuro The way we use our brain.

Neuro-linguistic programming (NLP) Defined as the study of the structure of subjective experience. The name was developed by John Grinder and Richard Bandler in 1975. It is a process of modeling and increasingly the term is used to encompass the techniques and skills uncovered as a result of this process.

Outcome (well formed) A goal that is characteristic of someone who consistently achieves what they want in ways that are a *win* for others as well as themselves. Different from traditional methods of goal setting in that it involves the use of all senses, including emotion.

Pacing Respecting the values, the needs and the style of another person in a way that leads to rapport. Going along with aspects of what is important to another and yourself.

Perceptual positions The mental strategy used by skillful negotiators involving moving mentally between being in your own shoes, the shoes of the other person and an outside, detached position. There is an old Indian saying: 'You must first walk two moons in a man's moccasins before you can understand him.'

Programming Not the computer kind but similar, in that it is to do with the sequences of thinking and behavior patterns that constitute our strategies for achieving the results we do.

Rapport Our ability to relate to ourselves and others in ways that create a climate of respect, trust and cooperation.

Reframing The ability to make meanings of events in ways that work for you and create desirable emotional states.

State The mental, physical and emotional condition of a person.

Strategies A set of thinking and behavioral steps to achieve a result.

TOTE (test–operate–test–exit) The feedback loop used to guide behavior.

Well-formed outcomes *See* outcomes.

Taking your learning further

*T*HE Sue Knight Partnership is one of the leading organizations offering business and personal development-related programs and public courses in NLP in the world today. They specialize in leadership training and development.

The Sue Knight Partnership runs public courses leading to business certification in NLP. They are:

Personal Mastery A comprehensive introduction to NLP, covering the material that is included in the book NLP *at Work*.

Leadership for the Future A modular course leading to certification as a Business Practitioner in NLP. Modules cover the themes of High Performance Coaching, Managing Change, Strategies for Success and the Learning Organization as well as Personal Development.

Pioneering Excellence An advanced course in modeling skills leading to certification in NLP. This course is a practical experience of the skills and concepts covered in this book.

Free open afternoons
The Sue Knight Partnership regularly hold free open afternoons where you can meet the team of associates and experience some of the NLP skills in action.

In-company work
The Sue Knight team will meet with you to discuss how they might help you with any in-company training and development and to agree outcomes for the work they do.

To find out more or to receive an information pack, contact:

The Sue Knight Partnership
PO Box 1008
Slough, SL1 8DB
UK

Telephone: +44 (0)1628 667868
Fax: +44 (0)1628 667865
E-mail: sue@sueknight.co.uk
Web page: www.sueknight.co.uk